PAUL
the
COUNSELOR

Counseling and Disciple-making
Modeled by the Apostle

Edited by
Mark Shaw & Bill Hines

Paul the Counselor:
Counseling and Disciple-making Modeled by the Apostle

Edited by Mark Shaw and Bill Hines

Copyright 2014

Cover Design by Melanie Schmidt

ISBN: 978-1-936141-25-8

Printed in the United States of America
Focus Publishing
PO Box 665
Bemidji, MN 56619

DEDICATION

With gratefulness to God we dedicate this work to

Dr. Howard A. Eyrich

His life as a child of God, husband, father,
grandfather, pastor, teacher and counselor has been
an exhibition of the godly pursuit of holiness. As
one who loves God and others, he has given us an
example of the sufficiency of God's Word for all
of life's challenges and joys. We are blessed to call
him Mentor and Friend.

Mark Shaw and Bill Hines

ACKNOWLEDGEMENTS

As in all our works we stand on the shoulders of those theologians, Bible teachers and counselors from whom we have learned by the power of the Holy Spirit. They are too numerous to name. We would, however, like to thank Jan Haley for her vision for the completion of this book, along with Andrea Heck and Sherry Haley, for the editing which is quite a task for a multi-authored work. We also thank Melanie Schmidt for her time in formatting the design of the book.

We are grateful for our wives, Mary Shaw and Kathy Hines, who share our vision to provide help to those who are hurting, and to those who help them. Their love, vision and encouragement are central to all that we do.

We thank God for allowing each of the authors of this work to have a glimpse of the glory to be revealed when we are united with Christ, and pray that He will be glorified in the use of the words printed here. To Him we offer our praise and lives.

Mark Shaw and Bill Hines

TABLE OF CONTENTS

Introduction
PAUL'S ADMONITION TO CHRISTLIKENESS

Mark Shaw and Bill Hines

Him we proclaim, warning everyone and teaching everyone with all wisdom, that we may present everyone mature in Christ.
Colossians 1:28

The Apostle Paul described his ministry in Asia saying, **". . . I did not shrink from declaring to you anything that was profitable, and teaching you in public and from house to house."** Paul reflects his boldness by demonstrating how he took every opportunity to preach, teach, and counsel in the ministry of the Word of God in both public preaching of the Word and private "house to house" ministry. We often call this house to house ministry disciple-making or biblical counseling. Paul was a minister of the Gospel because he dealt with sin and proclaimed Christ as Savior for repentant sinners.

As a counselor, Paul addressed sin and responsibility before God to those to whom he ministered. He could have been given many titles during his very active ministry: Paul the Preacher, the Disciple-maker, the Pastor, the Shepherd, the Missionary, the Apologist, the Author, the Public Figure, the Laborer in the kingdom of God, and more. In all of this, Paul counseled, and in this book we want to examine how he carried on this aspect of disciple-making as a personal ministry of the sufficient Word of God.

Each of the contributing authors in this book will demonstrate the wisdom of the Word of God directly from the scriptural writings of the Apostle Paul. They will address how Paul discipled his counselees by blessing and comforting them, teaching them how to change through the help of the Holy Spirit, helping them deal with temptation, demonstrating how to find freedom in the new man, and addressing many other issues pertaining to living life in a fallen world. This is essentially what is known today as biblical counseling. The same wisdom that Paul applied from the Word and the same power from the Holy Spirit upon which he relied are available to the biblical counselor today.

1

Our hope is that you will be able to apply Paul's methods and impart God's counsel to those whom God has entrusted to your care. Pastors, counselors, teachers, and lay leaders are all responsible for caring for souls within the Body of Christ. God has sovereignly placed husbands, wives, grandparents, parents, children, uncles, aunts, and trusted Christian friends in your life who will be constantly presenting you with relational opportunities to speak the truth in love. In this volume, you will find sound wisdom and practical teaching from the Bible.

So how did Paul counsel? In Colossians 1:28 above, notice the word **warning,** which is also translated "admonishing" in some Bible translations.[1] Warning and admonishing are interesting, rich words full of scriptural meaning and application. Some translate **warning** as "counseling," but the concept is more than what our culture usually implies by the word "counseling." Of the Apostle Paul's use of this word, William Hendriksen says: "For [Paul] to admonish meant to warn, to stimulate and to encourage. He would actually plead with people to be reconciled to God (2 Corinthians 5:20). He would at times even shed tears (Acts 20:19, 31; 2 Corinthians 2:4; Philippians 4:18)."[2] To warn people is to save them from the further agony of their sin. Stimulating them is to "stir up" or "agitate" within them the desire to pursue Christ-likeness. To encourage is to give them hope in a God of grace to fulfill His promises to His children. To engage in a ministry that seeks to warn, to stimulate, and to encourage people to Christ-likeness is to do the work of compassionate biblical counseling.[3]

Who is to counsel according to God's Word? Is counseling reserved only for those who know the Scriptures exceedingly well, like the Apostle Paul? The answer may surprise some, for it is our understanding from Scripture that all Christians are to counsel some of the time. This comes from passages such as:

---

1   The remaining paragraphs of this introduction are adapted from *Curing the Heart* by William Hines and Howard Eyrich (Mentor Publishing).

2   Hendriksen, William, *New Testament Commentary: Philippians, Colossians, and Philemon*, (Grand Rapids: Baker Book House, 1985).

3   The word or its root translated "warning" or "admonishing" here is also used in the following passages: Acts 20:31; Romans 15:14; 1 Corinthians 4:14; Colossians 1:28; Colossians 3:16; 1 Thessalonians 5:12, 14; 2 Thessalonians 3:15.

- **Brothers, if anyone is caught in any transgression, you who are spiritual should restore him in a spirit of gentleness. Keep watch on yourself, lest you too be tempted** (Galatians 6:1). Here, those who are spiritual or those who have some maturity as Christians should help restore the sinner.[4] This is a work that would be expected of the biblical counselor.

- **But you are a chosen race, a royal priesthood, a holy nation, a people for his own possession, that you may proclaim the excellencies of him who called you out of darkness into his marvelous light....** (1 Peter 2:9). Here, Christians are referred to as a royal priesthood. The priest is one who represents the people to God and God to the people. All Christians are priests and we all have a responsibility to intercede on behalf of our brothers and sisters. This is one aspect of the work of counseling. It should also be noted that this is not an option for the Christian. Again, we are each priests and therefore we are to do the work of a priest, which is to minister the Word of God in a private, "house to house" manner.

Paul further supports this as he addresses the Christians in Rome as those he considered able to do the work of counseling discipleship in Romans 15:14: **I myself am satisfied about you, my brothers, that you yourselves are full of goodness, filled with all knowledge and able to instruct one another.** Notice that Paul is addressing not only the leaders, but also the rank and file brethren. He is satisfied with them, but notice what he is satisfied about. He is confident that all three of these characteristics are present and at work within them. One without the other would nullify the effectiveness of the other two.

Biblical truth is fully realized by knowing the God of truth. It is one thing to know of sacrifice, but until we personally come to grips with the devastation of our own sin and our utter dependence on the mercy of God to save sinners, experiential knowledge of the sacrifice of the Savior is incomplete. Goodness, for example, is the attribute of one who is others-oriented; what he does is for the benefit of others. Goodness looks intently for an opening to be helpful. It is

---

4   See 1 Corinthians 2:15, 3:1-3 for a discussion on spirituality. In these passages we find that a spiritual person is one who 1) possesses the Spirit, and 2) has achieved some level of maturity.

listed as one characteristic of the fruit of the Spirit (Galatians 5:22). We stress this aspect of goodness being linked to knowledge because it is vital. Counsel *without* biblical truth delivered from the heart of the fellow Pilgrim, even one who has ever-increasing wisdom of the Spirit of God in his heart, is a hymn of death. It tickles the ears at best and delivers a message of evil because it does not deliver the message of God. Instruction brings biblical knowledge and the heart of goodness to bear on the issue of discipleship. Instruction is "wisdom as we walk" (see Deuteronomy 6:4-9). Therefore, according to Paul, a Christian who is full of goodness and knowledge will be able to instruct or *admonish* another.

So what does it mean to biblically admonish, instruct, or counsel? In our day, counseling is often the idea of someone caring, listening reflectively, or giving advice that helps people feel better. Many modern therapists warn their counseling students against telling people what to do. They think that to be directive is to impose on the person some external truth and that it is better for the person to "find" or discover the truth within themselves. That is not the biblical idea of helping. There is absolute truth, and people come to counselors because they need to know answers and they do not have them. We need to care enough to tell them the truth. This is at the heart of our biblical definition and we find it again expressed by the apostle Paul in his letter to the Colossians: **Him we proclaim, warning everyone and teaching everyone with all wisdom, that we may present everyone mature in Christ** (Colossians 1:28). Our prayer is that you will live and counsel as Paul the Counselor did, proclaiming Christ alone as the sufficient answer to all counseling problems, and both warning and teaching your counselees and acquaintances with all wisdom that they might grow into mature believers for the glory of God alone.

PERSONAL CONNECTION QUESTIONS

1. Who are the people and what are the ministry opportunities in your life now? Consider some of the persons God has placed in your life who need salvation, and some who are already Christians but still need a personal ministry of disciple-making in order to grow into Christ-likeness.

2. Action Assignment: Make a list of three persons you can begin meeting with regularly for prayer and Bible study and then contact them in the next week to begin doing so. Meet daily, weekly, bi-weekly, or once per month, but begin meeting for intentional, relational disciple-making.

Notes

Chapter 1
PAUL AND DISCIPLE-MAKING

Mark Shaw

> So Barnabas went to Tarsus to look for Saul, and
> when he had found him, he brought him to Antioch.
> For a whole year they met with the church and taught
> a great many people. And in Antioch the disciples
> were first called Christians.
>
> Acts 11:25-26

Sometimes, when we read the Bible, we think that a man as gifted as the Apostle Paul was instantly used by God in mighty ways because of his natural God-given abilities. However, we find in the verses above that Paul (whose name was Saul) was sought after by a man named Barnabas who brought Paul to Antioch and the two of them ministered together for an entire year. Though not explicit in the Scriptures, it appears that Barnabas was discipling Paul while actively doing ministry together as a team. When I read those verses, I always wonder, "What did they do together? What type of training did Paul receive? What was Barnabas' curriculum or 'program of discipleship' that he used with Paul that cultivated Paul's gifts?" Whatever Barnabas did, it was fruitful as evidenced by the impact that Paul's ministry is having even to this day. The "disciples were first called Christians," or "little Christs," a derogatory term likely devised by pagans, but it is a true reflection of one of the goals of disciple-making: to become like Christ.

In this chapter, we will examine how the Apostle Paul obeyed the call of Jesus Christ to be a disciple-maker in Matthew 28:18-20:

> And Jesus came and said to them, "All authority
> in Heaven and on earth has been given to me. Go
> therefore and make disciples of all nations, baptizing
> them in the name of the Father and of the Son and
> of the Holy Spirit, teaching them to observe all that
> I have commanded you. And behold, I am with you
> always, to the end of the age."

We will compare Paul's method of disciple-making with the three primary ways that disciples are taught to obey the Word of God: pulpit preaching, small group meetings, and personal ministry (which includes biblical counseling).

A Pyramid of Disciple-Making

Though disciple-making comes in many shapes and sizes today, it can be categorized into three basic areas based upon the number of participants: pulpit ministry, small group ministry, and personal ministry. Most Christians grow spiritually when they are involved simultaneously in all three areas of the inverted pyramid pictured here:

All three means of disciple-making in the local church pictured in the inverted pyramid rely upon the same source of truth in God's Word and the power of the Holy Spirit to bring transformation (Romans 12:1-2). Like Paul, all Christians want to be used in mighty ways by God. Knowledge of the Bible is good, but it is not enough. A believer must learn how to "do" the Bible or, in other words, live it out in their lives. James 1:22 states: **But be doers of the word, and not hearers only, deceiving yourselves.** Wisdom comes through the "doing" of God's Word and disciple-making is the tool Christ commanded His followers to use in **"teaching them to observe all that I have commanded you"** (Matthew 28:20).

One of the goals then is for Christians to **observe** or "obey" the commands of Christ. The disciples of Christ are to go and make disciples by baptizing and teaching them to obey His commands. It is not enough to simply hear the truth; we must heed the truth. Many Christians in the church today are hearing the Word of God preached but not putting it into practice. While hearing sermons is an important facet of the Christian life, it is not the only piece of the pyramid. It often involves little or no relational intimacy between the preacher and the listener. The preacher may open his heart but the listener is not required to do so.

Small groups offer more intimacy between the participants, yet some Christians will not be open about their struggles in even a small group setting. Those believers prefer a one-to-one disciple-making relationship to address their struggles of faith, living life in a fallen world, and navigating trials.

Personal disciple-making is a necessity for every Christian. The reasoning behind this strong statement is simple: mankind has a fallen, sinful nature that tends to please self above all others. For this reason, Christians need their own local body of Christ to both shepherd and support them (1 Peter 5:2-4; Hebrews 10:24-25). These aspects of the local church are commanded and expected. So, why do many families of faith neglect shepherding and personal ministry today? The answer is that personal ministry is often time-consuming, strenuous, and expensive. A church culture has emerged that longs to be amused rather than to be shepherded or to serve. When problems arise in a Christian's life, few leaders are equipped to address them biblically and even fewer are willing to invest the resources necessary (especially time) to bring about change.

Biblical Counseling: A Subset of Personal Ministry

The biblical counseling and relational disciple-making as modeled by Paul and Barnabas in Acts 11:25-26 presses believers to participate in the increasing practice of obedience to the Word of God in everyday life situations. As mentioned in the introduction, Paul writes in Acts 20:20, that **. . . I did not shrink from declaring to you anything that was profitable, and teaching you in public and from house to house.** Paul learned to minister the Word both publically and privately from house to house. Today, that type of personal ministry might include what is called "biblical counseling," which fits inside the inverted pyramid under the personal ministry heading.

Since it can be either formal or informal in its context, biblical counseling is only one small subset of the personal ministry of disciple-making. Formal biblical counseling happens in the local church under the authority of the "under-shepherds" and leaders of the faith family. Informal biblical counseling occurs between two Christians who may either be in an equal peer relationship (like friend to friend) or in a mentor-mentee relationship (like an older woman teaching a younger woman or a parent teaching a child). It always involves at least two people, the Holy Spirit, and the Word of God.

Hearing sermons is good for all believers. Even more effective is hearing sermons from the pulpit as well as sermons in a biblical counseling session with weekly accountability. One of the advantages of disciple-making through biblical counseling is that 1 Thessalonians 5:14 can be applied specifically to a person: **And we urge you, brothers, admonish the idle, encourage the fainthearted, help the weak, be patient with them all.** Skilled biblical counselors can discern differences among those whom they are counseling: the idle, fainthearted, or weak. Each of these three categories of persons requires a different type of counsel. The idle need admonishment, the fainthearted need encouragement, and the weak need help. All of them require patience from the personal minister who can be any Christian in the local church!

While a sermon may provide all three (the idle, fainthearted, and weak) with the type of counsel they need, a personal ministry relationship of biblical counseling is more likely to provide each with the specific counsel required from the Word of God. Personal ministry will hit the "target," which is the heart of the counselee. That is why some call biblical counseling "pin-pointed discipleship," because it is like a special operations unit in the armed forces designed to attack the enemy in a specific, focused way. Preaching is often more general since it has a bigger audience, while a personal ministry of the Word can be more specific because of the smaller audience.

Paul and Barnabas conducted their ministries in this relational model of disciple-making as they lived life together and sharpened each other while accomplishing the goals of ministry set before them. They were successful in ministry, advancing God's kingdom agenda to reach the lost Gentile world for Christ.

How Paul Learned to Disciple

Barnabas, whose name means "son of encouragement," (Acts 4:26) defended and endorsed Paul (who was still named Saul at that time) to the early believers because of Paul's shady past as a killer of Christians: **But Barnabas took him and brought him to the apostles and declared to them how on the road he had seen the Lord, who spoke to him, and how at Damascus he had preached boldly in the name of Jesus** (Acts 9:27). With confidence, Barnabas testified to the transforming power of Christ in the life of Saul in order to free him to preach boldly in Jerusalem (Acts 9:28). Then Paul spent a year working with Barnabas in Antioch, a cosmopolitan city that became the sending church for mission work in Asia and Europe. Again, the Scriptures do not explicitly say that Barnabas was discipling Paul, but it is interesting to note that every time the two of them are mentioned by the author (Luke) prior to Acts 13:9, the Bible lists them as "Barnabas and Saul" with Barnabas listed first. In Acts 13:9 Saul's name officially changed to Paul: **But Saul, who was also called Paul, filled with the Holy Spirit, looked intently at him . . .** From that point forward, the Bible consistently calls them "Paul and Barnabas."[5]

Barnabas was a successful disciple-maker with his student Paul, who became a Christ-like leader using his own God-given gifts to advance the kingdom of God. In churches focused solely on the pulpit ministry of the Word, it is easy to sometimes miss the relational context of disciple-making, which is a personal ministry of the Word. Biblical training and education are important slices of the pie for a Christ-follower, but remember that knowledge puffs up and love builds up. Because of Paul's upbringing as a Pharisee (Philippians 3:5), we know that he was well-educated (1 Corinthians 8:1), so his intention in working with Barnabas for a year was not to gain a degree. In the same model that Christ utilized (Luke 10:1), Paul was paired with Barnabas in a ministerial relationship that refined and directed Paul's zeal of expanding the kingdom of God into the uncharted territory of the Gentiles.

---

5   Acts 15:12 and 15:25 are the two exceptions where Barnabas is listed before Paul, but even those instances are evidence of the respect the writer has for Barnabas as a leader and disciple-maker.

Proverbs 27:17 describes their relationship well: **Iron sharpens iron, and one man sharpens another.** Barnabas as the disciple-maker grew spiritually in his relationship with Paul, too, until the two of them parted ways in Acts 15. Interestingly, when Paul and Barnabas separated, each of them took another man along with them: Paul chose Silas and Barnabas chose John Mark (Acts 15:36-41). Although much is made of the disagreement Paul and Barnabas had in Acts 15, God used it as an opportunity for two more men to be discipled by Paul and Barnabas. We know that Paul also discipled Timothy, Luke, and Titus so there is a pattern of relational, two-by-two disciple-making established in the New Testament.

Jesus Himself sent out His followers in teams of two for mutual strength and encouragement in Luke 10:1-3:

> **After this the Lord appointed seventy-two others and sent them on ahead of him, two by two, into every town and place where he himself was about to go. And he said to them, "The harvest is plentiful, but the laborers are few. Therefore pray earnestly to the Lord of the harvest to send out laborers into his harvest. Go your way; behold, I am sending you out as lambs in the midst of wolves."**

The beauty of Jesus' model of ministry is found in greater wisdom, love, and replication of disciples. Unlike worldly culture, which often emphasizes individualism even in the church, Jesus, Paul, and Barnabas emphasized relational disciple-making by doing ministry together with at least one other person.

In Matthew 28:19-20, the disciples were not commanded to "Sit therefore and listen to sermons," but were given a mandate to **"Go therefore and make disciples of all nations . . . teaching them to observe all that I have commanded you."** We have too many "sitters and soakers" who make excuses for not making disciples when there are no acceptable excuses, because this is a command of Christ. Paul and Barnabas obeyed the command to go, and they then made more disciples of all nations. The disciples they made were disciple-makers who produced disciple-makers who produced disciple-makers, and so on. The world has never been the same.

Today, the church must reclaim the relational element of making disciples and caring for souls. Pulpit ministry is a good start, but it is not enough. As we saw in the last chapter, Paul ministered the Word both publically and privately (Acts 20:20). Many churches are strong in the pulpit (public proclamation of the Word) yet struggle in the private (one to one, or house to house) proclamation of the Word. Members do not know how to live out the Word in their personal lives, marriages, and families. They hear a solid sermon each week and participate in small group activities, but the intimate "iron sharpening iron" area of disciple-making is too often non-existent. In family life, crisis marital situations abound as a result. The wife is ready to leave her husband in divorce and the pastor and church are shocked because outwardly no one saw any "signs."

In these cases, professing Christians are like the foolish man described by Jesus in Matthew 7:26-27:

> **And everyone who hears these words of mine and does not do them will be like a foolish man who built his house on the sand. And the rain fell, and the floods came, and the winds blew and beat against that house, and it fell, and great was the fall of it.**

The Apostle Paul was a man who weathered more than a few "storms" in his life (2 Corinthians 11:24-28) and did not fall because of God's mighty hand. He spent relational time learning to do ministry and to become like Christ, placing his faith and confidence in the Almighty. Our culture desperately needs men and women who are discipled to stand through the trials of life to reflect the glory of God in a fallen, sin-cursed world. Biblical counseling provides opportunities to renew the mind by helping Christian counselees learn what God says in His Word and how to practically implement it for the glory of God.

Followers of Christ need the preaching of the Word, small group fellowships within the faith family centered upon the Word and prayer, and the personal ministry of intimate disciple-making centered upon the Word and prayer (included is counseling that is biblical). These are not optional areas for the believer today. There are too many worldly influences, temptations of Satan, and sinful tendencies in our flesh to take our Christian walk lightly. Christians must be renewed in their minds by the Holy Spirit and the Word of God, which best happens in disciple-making relationships.

All believers need to be discipled and to become disciple-makers, even if only in their own families. We live in urgent times and are in a spiritual battle, whether we realize it or not. Our children, friends, and family relationships need biblical truth to saturate their thinking and they need relational disciple-making to learn how to obediently apply the Scriptures in their everyday lives in order to fulfill the command of Christ in Matthew 28:18-20.

Following the Model of Christ

Jesus focused the majority of His time in relational disciple-making and He did so according to the inverted pyramid we saw earlier. First, Jesus "counseled" many of those who followed Him in a formal way, like Peter in Matthew 16, and in informal, personal conversations with those He encountered like the woman at the well in John 4 and the rich young ruler of Mark 10. Jesus developed three key leaders in Peter, James, and John, who have had a major impact upon the modern Christian church. Jesus implemented the personal ministry of biblical counseling to Peter several times as recorded in Scripture. One instance is in Matthew 16:21-23:

> **From that time Jesus began to show his disciples that he must go to Jerusalem and suffer many things from the elders and chief priests and scribes, and be killed, and on the third day be raised. And Peter took him aside and began to rebuke him, saying, "Far be it from you, Lord! This shall never happen to you." But he turned and said to Peter, "Get behind me, Satan! You are a hindrance to me. For you are not setting your mind on the things of God, but on the things of man."**

It was necessary for Jesus to rebuke Peter for thinking in a worldly and even satanic manner, yet we know that Jesus graciously counseled Peter by speaking the truth in love to him, since Jesus was **"full of grace and truth"** (John 1:14). Peter needed Jesus' wise counsel and admonishment because he was thinking in an ungodly way. This "biblical counsel" Jesus gave to Peter in their disciple-making relationship was vital to Peter's proper understanding of God. The personal ministry of biblical counseling in the pyramid picture was accomplished by Jesus in this passage and in many others.

The second part of the pyramid, called "small groups" was accomplished by Jesus as He devoted time to train all twelve of His disciples in the moments of life that they shared together. In Matthew 10, Jesus called His disciples to Him and then sent them out with instructions for ministry. He trained the twelve disciples within their small group and their teaching from Him in this context was conducted in private since it was directed to them specifically as a group.

The third part of the pyramid is clear as we always recall how Jesus preached the Word to the multitudes around Him. He ministered to large crowds by teaching them to apply the Word. What is known as the "Sermon on the Mount" in Matthew 5-7 is an excellent example of biblical disciple-making by Jesus to the large crowds, and many churches follow this example today in large worship gatherings. The public proclamation of the Word is a vital portion of the pyramid of disciple-making in the faith family, but it is not the only method. The Holy Spirit intentionally works for spiritual growth and God's glory in each of the three areas of the inverted pyramid: preaching, small groups, and personal ministry.

Conclusion

Like Jesus, the Apostle Paul utilized the same pyramid in making disciples. We know that Paul preached boldly (Acts 9:28; 20:20), ministered to the brothers in a small group setting (Acts 17:10-15), and provided counsel to Timothy in both of his letters addressed directly to him (1 Timothy and 2 Timothy). Paul ministered by utilizing all three portions of the pyramid, planted thriving churches, and discipled faithful men to be not only disciples of Christ, but disciple-makers.

Our encouragement to you is to implement Paul's model of disciple-making, especially through the personal ministry of biblical counseling. Not everyone is gifted or called to a pulpit ministry but everyone is called to minister the Word of God by living in community and making disciples in a personal way with those persons God has placed around you. You are commanded to make disciples who will follow Jesus Christ and not follow you or your best ideas (Matthew 28:18-20). They need to know God as He has revealed Himself through Jesus Christ and His written Word, the Bible, for the purpose of being renewed in their thinking. Quite likely their thinking has been unbiblical, and you are to teach them to obey God by doing what His Word teaches.

You can be an instrument God will use to provide grace in the lives of those you disciple. Who knows? You may disciple just one person to follow Christ and, like Barnabas, your obedience to Christ and His Word may produce someone zealous like the Apostle Paul! 2 Timothy 2:1-2 best summarizes Paul's relational approach to disciple-making:

> **You then, my child, be strengthened by the grace that is in Christ Jesus, and what you have heard from me in the presence of many witnesses entrust to faithful men who will be able to teach others also.**

PERSONAL CONNECTION QUESTIONS

1. Did you contact one of the three persons listed in the Action Assignment of the Introduction chapter of this book? If not, then contact one of them or a leader in your church to meet with you regularly for the purpose of the personal ministry of biblical counseling and disciple-making. Ask them to commit time to you (weekly is ideal) and tell them that you in return will submit to the Word of God that they share with you. No one wants to enter into a disciple-making relationship with a person who is not going to implement the Word of God in their lives for lasting change, so take this commitment seriously.

2. Listen to your disciple-maker and make practical changes in your life. The Word of God is the truth that we submit to and that Word is often delivered by a human being. Submission in a disciple-making relationship is the key to success. You are ultimately submitting to Christ and His Word, no matter who the person is delivering the truth. For example, let's pretend that my son says to me in a respectful, soft, and gracious tone of voice, "Dad, the Bible says that our words are to build each other up (Ephesians 4:29). Are your words to me building up or tearing down?" My response must not be: "Son, you are a child. I don't listen to you or obey you. Now go to your room. I am the parent." No! My response to what he is saying must be, "Son, thank you for loving me and reminding me of the truth of God's Word. I will change my words and tone immediately in obedience to God." The vessel, or person, through which the Word of God is delivered, is not what I am submitting to; I am submitting to God ultimately and to His Word of truth.

3.   Action Assignment: Find one to three persons willing to allow you to become their disciple-maker and begin meeting with them weekly to disciple them for the purpose of their spiritual growth in Christ. Your meetings can simply be a time of sitting down, opening the Word, reading it out loud, and applying it to your lives in a specific manner.

Chapter 2
PAUL AND SIN

David M. Tyler and Alonza Jones

Or do you not know that the unrighteous will not inherit the kingdom of God? Do not be deceived: neither the sexually immoral, nor idolaters, nor adulterers, nor men who practice homosexuality, nor thieves, nor the greedy, nor drunkards, nor revilers, nor swindlers will inherit the kingdom of God. And such were some of you. But you were washed, you were sanctified, you were justified in the name of the Lord Jesus Christ and by the Spirit of our God.
1 Corinthians 6:9-11

In the world today, there is nothing that more fully deserves to be abhorred and condemned than sin. Sin drove our first parents out of paradise (Genesis 3) and brought unnumbered miseries upon the whole human race. There is turmoil everywhere; war, bloodshed, rivalries and cruelties of all descriptions. Nations and peoples are working against one another in strife. You cannot read the morning paper or watch the evening news without being reminded of the trials, wretchedness, and unhappiness in the world.

Because of sin, our personal lives are full of difficulties, and we are often overwhelmed by them. Life is full of misunderstandings, jealousies, and discord. There are always problems, disappointments, or illnesses. People struggle within themselves and look for ways out of their predicaments to find love, joy, and peace; yet these things are only found in Christ as we learn to obey His Word.

Understanding God and His Word

The Bible is a very practical book. Unfortunately, many people and even some Christians believe that the Bible is too distant and archaic to address the "real" problems in life. This is especially true in so-called "Christian" counseling, which believes the Scriptures are insufficient and must be supplemented by secular ideas and their atheistic models. However, nothing could be further from the truth. The whole purpose of God's Word is to provide salvation, or newness of life, by instructing and enlightening us concerning the very situations in which we find ourselves.

As a practical source book for the problems we face, the Bible provides solutions to resolve relational conflict with God and others. Just as the owner's manual in a car provides diagnostic help with mechanical problems, the Bible addresses problems honestly and provides new patterns of thinking so that problems may be rightly considered in our minds. In Genesis 3 we find the first recorded "problem" in the Bible (the fall of Adam and Eve). In Genesis 4 another problem arises between Cain and God and then Cain and his brother Abel. Interpersonal problems and conflict continue in the Bible between Joseph and his brothers, Jacob and Esau, David and Saul, and many others. In the New Testament, every person Jesus encountered had some type of problem. In fact, the New Testament epistles were written because of problems that confronted the early church. Men and women with problems are on every page of Scripture, and where did they turn? They turned to God and His people as they trusted His Word of truth to be sufficient to address their problems.

In James 4:1-10, the Bible talks honestly to us about why we are miserable. What is the cause of our unhappiness and difficulties? Why do things go wrong? Why are there adulteries, fornication, murders, deceit, jealousies and disease? Why is there death? There is one common denominator, and that is sin. The Bible is not detached and theoretical but poignant and practical, in that it directs us to our own desires which are saturated in sin (James 4:3-4). The Bible comes to us and says, "I want to talk to you about *you*. Why are you having difficulties? Why are you anxious and depressed?" The truths found in the Bible are indispensable to understanding ourselves and the world in which we live.

In the Beginning

How are we to understand ourselves and our problems? The Bible starts in Genesis 1:1 with **"In the beginning God . . ."** Immediately, we recognize a distinction with respect to other secular and non-Christian religious views about life. All other views begin and end with man. The Bible, in order to understand man, begins with God.

The biblical counselor must begin with Him, too.

For this reason, it is necessary to come to an accurate understanding of God for the purpose of knowing Him intimately so that we may trust Him. Before asking yourself questions centered upon you and your problems, you must start with knowing God as He reveals Himself in His Word. People mistakenly want to start with their problems, and in so doing they fail to see the larger picture. They fail to put life in its proper *context* of a fallen, sin-cursed world with sin-stained people. The only way to truly understand oneself and begin to make sense of life is to start with God. Does the universe exist as a result of the activity of God or blind chance? Are we created entities by a supernatural, divine Person or the result of the accidental and purposeless collision of atoms?

The Bible puts life in its truthful context of a sinfully fallen world and then addresses and answers the particulars of our situations with biblical principles to be applied for the glory of Christ. Unlike biblical counseling, secular psychological counseling starts with you and ends with you. Man is the alpha and omega in psychological theories not based upon the Word of God. These theorists suggest your situation is due to the environment, childhood experiences, DNA, dysfunctional family, or low self-esteem, but never a sinful attitude problem. The secular counselor proposes ideas not based in Scripture to the counselee and suggests certain medications and life skills to implement. The whole effort in secular counseling is focused upon fixing a person. Presupposing evolution to be true, the secular counselor's efforts to truly understand man are futile when devoid of God. The Bible teaches us that human beings cannot be understood until we rightly see God as our Sovereign Maker and Owner.

When the Bible talks about mankind, however, it doesn't start with your problems but begins by placing you in the right context in Genesis 1:1: **In the beginning God . . . Then God said, "Let Us make man in Our image and according to Our likeness . . ."** In your attempt to understand yourself and your problems, you must believe that there was a time when man was perfect. Man, made in the image of God, was righteous. It was a time when man enjoyed intimacy with God and communed with Him daily. There was no disease. There were no problems. There was no sin. The world was not like it is today.

Man was created by God for God. God placed man in a paradise called the Garden of Eden. There Adam and Eve lived a life of complete happiness (Genesis 1 & 2). Then why is man as he is today? Why is there so much misery and suffering? The Bible says that mankind disbelieved and disobeyed God's Word in Genesis 3 and it all started with a simple question designed to lead Adam and Eve to doubt God and His Word: **Now the serpent was more crafty than any beast of the field which the Lord God had made. And he said to the woman, "Indeed, has God said, 'You shall not eat from any tree of the garden?'"** (Genesis 3:1).

When starting with God as a solution to our problems, a counselee may object and say, "I am not interested in Bible stories. I am not interested in doctrine. I am full of trouble. My marriage is falling apart and I am depressed. Help me find relief for my problems." It is only as one rightly understands theology, however, that he can find real comfort and solutions to his problems. Theology teaches us that Satan, in the body of a serpent, entered into paradise and opposed God to deceive mankind (Genesis 3).

The Bible opens our understanding to know that that there is another world unlike ours: a spiritual world. God not only created man, but He created spiritual beings called angels. God endowed angels with remarkable powers to be servants. One angel, Lucifer, rebelled against his Creator and persuaded one third of all the angels of Heaven to follow him. God judged Lucifer, known now as Satan, and cast him to the earth.

The Bible teaches that this horrible, powerful being commonly called Satan then entered God's perfect world and tempted Adam and Eve, God's crowning creation. Adam and Eve's sinful choice to disbelieve God while believing Satan's lies brought to pass all the terrible things you and I know and experience now in this world. This explains why man is different from what he once was. Mankind is in the grip of this evil power because of his own choices to obey the god of this world, Satan (2 Corinthians 4:4). Theology calls this original sin.

Original sin teaches us about our sinful nature. Original sin is why all alternative remedies to our problems are hopeless and inadequate at bringing real transformation. They do not take into account the unseen forces in human life brought on by a sinful nature also called our "flesh." Secular psychology discounts sin as though it is simply a "mistake" or some action that a person occasionally does that society deems as wrong. Psychology ignores the spiritual battle everyone experiences. But Paul said . . . **for our struggle is not against flesh and blood, but against the rulers, against the powers, against the world forces of this darkness, against the spiritual forces of wickedness in the heavenly places** (Ephesians 6:12).

Psychology says it is only flesh and blood that we struggle against: disease, disorders, addictions, chemical imbalances, and so on. All the explanations are materialistic and focused on this life rather than upon eternity with God our Creator. There is no room for God, angels, or fallen mankind in their theories devoid of truth. They incorrectly say that man is like an animal with instincts because he has gone through various stages of evolution from fish, reptile, and mammal. They theorize that mankind has not had sufficient time to completely shed the animal character to become the perfect man, but he is getting better and better.

But that view is wrong, according to the Bible. Realistically, the Bible tells us that the reason for all the problems in our lives and in the world is, ultimately, sin. Satan tempted man, and man willfully turned against his Creator and asserted himself in an attempt to become autonomous from God. Therefore, mankind is responsible and cannot blame Satan for his deception. Satan simply provided the bait, and mankind made the disobedient choice. The result was that God pronounced a curse on Satan, the woman, the man, and His created world.

Go and Sin No More

Man's basic problem is not that he has yet to evolve and reach his highest level of self-fulfillment and achievement. His problem is sin. To call the problem anything other than sin is to set the stage for applying solutions that are aimed at the wrong problem. What good is it to buy a taller ladder to scale a wall only to discover later that your ladder was leaning against the wrong wall? The right solution only works on the right problem.

As mentioned earlier in this chapter, the Bible is "problem-oriented." The Bible is also solution-oriented. For the balance of this chapter, we will discuss the Bible's straightforward, solution-oriented approach to sin.

You remember the old joke where the patient goes to his doctor, raises his arm up and down, and says, "Doctor, doctor! It hurts when I do this!" And the doctor says, "Well, then don't do that!" This silly and painfully lame joke may be more profound than you think. You see, the doctor perceived from the patient's words that his problem rested in the up-and-down movement of his arm. The logical fix for pain that comes from an up-and-down movement is to stop the up-and-down movement! The solution matches the perceived problem.

The same is true with human problems. For example, a drunkard should not be told that he is an "alcoholic" or that he is "self-medicating" when he drinks. Why? Because it would be a misrepresentation of his *real* problem. He is not sick with a so-called disease of "alcoholism." Rather, he has willfully developed the habit of drinking to the point of drunkenness rather than trusting God to be his **"very present help in trouble"** (Psalm 46:1). A thief is not a "kleptomaniac." She is someone who has willfully developed the habit of taking things that do not belong to her rather than turning to God as the one who supplies her every need (Philippians 4:19). Furthermore, sexual desire for someone of the same sex is not "gay" nor is it the "new normal." It is a choice that the Bible calls **"sexually immoral"** (1 Corinthians 6:9-10). What you call a thing really does matter. And how you label a problem will often dictate the type of solution offered.

In 1 Corinthians 6:9-11, Paul uses a label to describe a certain group of people. He calls unrighteous people "unrighteous." Here are his words: **Or do you not know that the unrighteous will not inherit the kingdom of God? Do not be deceived: neither the sexually immoral, nor idolaters, nor adulterers, nor men who practice homosexuality, nor thieves, nor the greedy, nor drunkards, nor revilers, nor swindlers will inherit the kingdom of God. And such were some of you. But you were washed, you were sanctified, you were justified in the name of the Lord Jesus Christ and by the Spirit of our God.**

Paul warned that unrepentant continuation in sin will result in being barred from the kingdom of God. It should be noted that Paul is not suggesting that born-again believers who sin will not inherit the kingdom of God. This would clearly be a contradiction of the overall teachings of Scripture and would fly in the face of the doctrine of sanctification. The word translated *unrighteous* is clearly a reference to unbelievers.

To be sure, Paul is writing to Christ-followers who, prior to their conversion, comfortably practiced the sins listed in this passage. Like Christians today, the Corinthian church continued to struggle with spiritual temptations and cultural pressures. As Christ-followers, our flesh will be with us until the day we exchange the **perishable** for the **imperishable** (1 Corinthians 15:53). However, we don't have to be defined by our sins. Because of our new nature, our past is not what we are. We do not have to daily say, "I am an alcoholic" but rather can say, "I am a redeemed drunkard by the blood of Christ."

Paul addressed sin in a way similar to the way in which Christ dealt with it during His earthly ministry. Paul's methodology will be examined. But first, let us take a glance back at an encounter Jesus had with a woman who had been caught in adultery. Here is the passage in its entirety:

> **But Jesus went to the Mount of Olives. Early in the morning He came again into the temple, and all the people were coming to Him; and He sat down and** *began* **to teach them. The scribes and the Pharisees brought a woman caught in adultery, and having set her in the center** *of the court*, **they said to Him, "Teacher, this woman has been caught in adultery, in the very act. Now in the Law Moses commanded us to stone such women; what then do You say?" They were saying this, testing Him, so that they might have grounds for accusing Him. But Jesus stooped down and with His finger wrote on the ground. But when they persisted in asking Him, He straightened up, and said to them, "He who is without sin among you, let him** *be the* **first to throw a stone at her." Again He stooped down and wrote on the ground. When they heard it, they** *began* **to go out one by one, beginning**

> **with the older ones, and He was left alone, and the woman, where she was, in the center** *of the court.* **Straightening up, Jesus said to her, "Woman, where are they? Did no one condemn you?" She said, "No one, Lord." And Jesus said, "I do not condemn you, either. Go. From now on sin no more** (John 8:1-11, NASB).

It is important to note that there is some debate as to whether this story was included in John's original account, since it cannot be found in the earliest manuscripts. Nevertheless, there is nothing in the passage that contradicts sound doctrine. Indeed, it contains a treasure trove of spiritual wisdom in how to properly address sin.

The Bible does not tell us a lot about this woman. Most of what we know about her was provided by the men who were ready to condemn her to death. While there is no evidence in these few verses that suggests she was being falsely accused, it is interesting that the other participant in the affair is not even mentioned.

We don't know her age. Neither do we know if she was married or pledged to be married; although this would have been a requirement under Jewish law in order for her to be stoned for adultery.

What we do know is that when Jesus addressed the woman, He didn't try to make her feel better about herself. He didn't blame her parents or the neighborhood in which she grew up. He didn't call what she did a "mistake." And, most importantly, He did not ignore her sin. He called her sin . . . sin, and said, *"sin* **no more."**

Jesus skipped the euphemisms. He didn't worry about being politically correct. In fact, He actually validated the claims of the woman's accusers. Jesus spoke the truth about this woman's problem and correctly called it *sin.*

Now, if Jesus had stopped at this point and walked away along with the others, His counsel to her would have been incomplete and, frankly, no different than what she had already received from the crowd. Instead of piously pointing out her sin in a finger-wagging tone, or unloading a barrage of do's and don'ts from the Bible, Jesus did something else: He helped her to see and accept the reality of her spiritual condition, and then He counseled her to reset and move forward in the power of a *new* spiritual condition.

Also, Jesus did not leave her there to wallow in self-pity and guilt. He forgave her—"I **do not condemn you, either,**"—He told her to **"Go."** Christ's compassionate, but unaltered, pronouncement of this woman's problem led to her humble submission to the right solution to her problem. Encouragement, while helpful, was not what she needed. She needed a new beginning. She needed a new heart. And that is precisely what she got from Jesus.

When Jesus asked, **"Woman, where are they? Did no one condemn you?"** she replied **"No one, Lord." "No one . . . ."** It was as if Jesus had just said, "Look. No one has condemned you!" And the woman's reply was not so much an answer as it was an echo of Jesus' words. She now saw in herself what Jesus saw. Then in humble adoration, she confirmed her new birth experience by calling Jesus "Lord." And while in the biblical records she will forever be known as the "woman caught in adultery," in the mind of Christ (and surely in her mind, as well), this woman will forever be known not as an adulterer but as a child of God . . . saint . . . one washed by the blood of the Lamb . . . a daughter of the King of kings and Lord of lords!

Before meeting Christ, this woman lay in the dirt accused, guilty, and condemned. After meeting Christ, she arose acquitted, forgiven, and redeemed. Might this marvelous conversion have happened had Christ addressed her sin problem as a sickness or a mere mistake? Hardly.

Like Christ, Paul did not sugarcoat the hard, but just, realities of sin. Neither did he excuse the sinner as a victim of societal circumstances. Regardless of the form in which it is manifested, sin's payoff will always be death (Romans 6:23). And those who continue in the unrepentant practice of sin will be excluded from the kingdom of God.

Biblical Labels Lead to New Life

In the 1 Corinthians 6 passage referenced earlier, Paul takes particular interest in nine specific sins. Now, we need to be careful here. The tendency of some might be to place heavier weight on this set of sins as compared to, say, less heinous ones (in terms of their consequences and societal judgments). But, when viewed within the broader context of the chapter, it becomes clear that the message Paul is trying to convey is that Christians are not only prone to behave just like unbelievers, they may find themselves being deceived into thinking that such sinful behavior is acceptable to God.

For example, they feel justified in dragging each other into secular court rooms rather than relying on church leaders to settle their disputes. Today, Christians would rather take each other to divorce court than seek reconciliation through wise biblical counseling from church elders. Likewise, Christians who don't want to appear "holier-than-thou" may be deceived into thinking that same-sex unions are fine as long as it is not called "marriage."

What if Paul's listing of these sins had nothing to do with the sins themselves? What if the Holy Spirit through Paul wanted the church at Corinth (and us) to see something far more significant in this passage? It would appear that this was indeed the case. A closer examination of Paul's methodology here reveals an unexpected focus. The emphasis is not on the past grievances of sinners. The emphasis of this passage is on the current grace of a Savior. Paul says . . . **And such *were* some of you. But you *were* washed, you *were* sanctified, you *were* justified in the name of the Lord Jesus Christ and by the Spirit of our God** (1 Corinthians 6:11, emphasis mine).

Note the use of past tense language. These believers are not being forced to relive their guilt-ridden pasts. Paul wants them to see who they *are*, not what they *were*. And that message is for you and me, as well.

Once we were stained by sin. Now we are clean because of the mercy of God (Titus 3:5). Once we were objects of God's wrath (Romans 1:18). Now we are set apart in Christ Jesus (1 Corinthians 1:2). Once we were guilty and condemned to hell. Now we are just and in a right standing with God (Romans 8:30). Paul's primary goal is to highlight the grace and mercy of God. He reminds us of our filthy, scandalous past to draw attention to the saving power of Christ's precious blood.

We live in a culture in which adultery is reviled when it is done in secret, but celebrated when it is done in the open on our TV screens. Celebrities can shoplift, drive drunk, and get arrested one week, and then land a starring role in a hit movie the next. And how many times have we seen reports of adult teachers having sex with minors only to have their actions excused as an "illness"?

Ours is a world in which right is wrong and wrong is right. Those for whom marriage *was* intended don't want to be married and those for whom marriage was *not* intended want to be married. Ours is a world that is, at once, horrified by the millions of unborn children who have been aborted and justified in our unwillingness to judge the perpetrators of these atrocities.

To be effective in ministering to the lost and to fellow believers who are living in disobedience, we must start by shining light on the real problem—sin—as the Apostle Paul did. The Gospel does not make sense without sin. And we must never, ever shrink back from applying the right solution to this problem—the Word of God.

PERSONAL CONNECTION QUESTIONS

1. Make three columns on a sheet of paper. In the far left column, write down a list of worldly terms that you often hear related to personal problems (i.e. alcoholic, having an affair, kleptomaniac, obsessive compulsive disorder). Then, in the middle column, write down the biblical alternative to each term listed in the left column. For the far right column, list Bible passages to support your answers in the middle column. Do this with a friend, family, children, co-workers and others.

2. How do you label your own sin? If you are not confronting your own sin regularly, you may be using incorrect, worldly terminology. Do a word study on anger, fear, worry, pride, and drunkenness to discover God's truth in dealing with these very real heart issues that are being re-labeled from "sin" to "sickness."

Notes

Chapter 3
PAUL AND TEMPTATION

Ed Bulkley

No temptation has overtaken you but such as is common to man; and God is faithful, who will not allow you to be tempted beyond what you are able, but with the temptation will provide the way of escape also, so that you will be able to endure it.
1 Corinthians 10:13, NASB

"I just couldn't help it! The temptation was just too great to overcome!" Every biblical counselor has heard this complaint and excuse time and again, in one form or another. It comes from those caught in multiple affairs of infidelity, people who are addicted to prescription drugs and alcohol, those who are obsessed with pornography, and others who have given themselves over to a variety of sins that dominate their lives.

Our psychologized culture has accepted the inevitability of failure and promotes perpetual victimization by following the disease model of personal weakness. One of the primary examples of this theory is the concept that "alcoholism" is a disease and not a result of personal choice or weakness. The theory has been around for centuries. Dr. Benjamin Rush, a signer of the Declaration of Independence, insisted that "habitual drunkenness should be regarded not as a bad habit but as a disease," calling it "a palsy of the will."

The disease model has spread beyond substance abuse to nearly every form of destructive behavior. Psychotherapists and lawyers have argued that those who engage in rape, murder, prostitution, torture, shoplifting, embezzlement, and unspeakable brutality are not really bad people. They simply can't control themselves, since they have diseased minds. Stanton Peele wrote the book, *Diseasing of America—How We Allowed Recovery Zealots and The Treatment Industry to Convince Us We are Out of Control,*[6] in which

---
6   Peele, Stanton, (NY, Lexington Books, 1995).

he lays out his conviction that our modern age has developed acute confusion in regard to the law, morality, and addictions.

Sadly, many who call themselves biblical counselors are equally confused and so anxious to receive professional acceptance that they have accommodated this worldly philosophy of irresponsibility. They have accepted the idea that no one is to be blamed for their thinking, attitudes, or behaviors, because diseased people simply can't control their minds, desires and actions. But can you imagine the Apostle Paul accepting such a philosophy?

When a member of the church of Corinth was guilty of a sexual sin that even scandalized unbelievers, Paul wrote, **It is actually reported that there is sexual immorality among you, and of a kind that does not occur even among pagans: A man has his father's wife**(1 Corinthians 5:1). Paul then commanded the church to respond quickly and decisively: **Expel the wicked man from among you** (1 Corinthians 5:13). Notice that he did not insist on the Corinthian church applying the Matthew 18 process of church discipline, since the sin was so obvious and damaging to the testimony of the church. Do you know why Paul was so firm in his discipline? It was because he was aware that **a little yeast works through the whole batch of dough** (1 Corinthians 5:6). Sin must be dealt with firmly, quickly, and biblically. There! I said it! I used that psychologically unacceptable word—*SIN*. But understanding that we are dealing with sin rather than disease is a vital component in helping your counselee to overcome temptation.

In writing this chapter, I am assuming that you, the reader, are a believer in Jesus Christ and that you want to please Him. You see, unless you have a desire to overcome temptation, we are both wasting our time. Victory begins with the desire to honor and obey the Lord. As David wrote, **"I rejoice in following your statutes as one rejoices in great riches"** (Psalm 119:14) and he made this commitment to the Lord: **"Give me understanding, and I will keep your law and obey it with all my heart"** (Psalm 119:34).

Understanding the Power of Sin

Let's examine, then, Paul's solution found in 1 Corinthians 10:13: **No temptation has overtaken you but such as is common to man;**

and God is faithful, who will not allow you to be tempted beyond what you are able, but with the temptation will provide the way of escape also, so that you will be able to endure it. First, let's examine what temptation *is*. The Greek word for temptation is *peirasmos* and it means "to prove" or "to undergo trial."[7] Temptation is something that tests and reveals one's character through a solicitation, enticement, or invitation to sin. The reason temptation is so difficult to resist is that it appeals to our desires; we *enjoy* sin, at least temporarily. Ultimately, it comes down to what we desire more—to please ourselves, or to please our Heavenly Father.

Paul continues in 1 Corinthians 10:13 by admitting that temptations can come unexpectedly: **"temptation has <u>seized</u> you"** (NIV, emphasis mine). A man can be innocently watching a football game with no thought of lust in his heart when suddenly the camera switches to the cheerleaders on the sideline who are doing their best to entice and to generate immoral desire. That is a perfect illustration of temptation taking or seizing a person unexpectedly. Temptation can and will come, and the wise child of God will prepare ahead of time.

Daniel, for instance, **purposed in his heart that he would not defile himself** (Daniel 1:8, KJV). His decision came *before* the temptation to compromise presented itself, and Daniel succeeded in his battle with sin. Job planned ahead as well: **"I made a covenant with my eyes not to look lustfully at a girl"** (Job 31:1, NIV). These were preemptive decisions. To defeat temptation, we must go on the offensive. Paul warns young Timothy to **flee from youthful lusts, and pursue righteousness, faith, love and peace, with those who call on the Lord from a pure heart** (2 Timothy 2:22). The point is that we must be on constant guard against temptation and actively pursue what is right. Peter emphasizes this truth when he writes, **Be self-controlled and alert. Your enemy the devil prowls around like a roaring lion looking for someone to devour** (1 Peter 5:8).

I once received a call from a church asking if I would be willing to counsel their pastor over a very serious matter. I agreed to do so, and when he came into my office he told me a tragic story of a woman

---

7   Strong, James, *The Exhaustive Concordance of the Bible: Showing Every Word of the Test of the Common English Version of the Canonical Books, and Every Occurrence of Each Word in Regular Order.*, electronic ed., G3986 (Ontario, Woodside Bible Fellowship, 1996).

in his congregation who determined she could entice any man she wanted, and she chose him as a target. The pastor knew she had a questionable reputation, yet when she invited him over to her house; he went alone, knowing full well what might follow. Temptation seized him and his testimony is now forever compromised; he is no longer the pastor of that church. Why? Because he forgot Paul's warning to **put on the Lord Jesus Christ, and make no provision for the flesh in regard to its lusts** (Romans 13:14, NASB).

Temptation is real, powerful, and insidious, but Paul reminds us that no temptation is unique: **No temptation has overtaken you but such as is <u>common to man</u>** (emphasis mine). This is important to understand, since we tend to think that our temptations are more difficult to overcome than those our neighbors' experience. The intense longing for cocaine high or the need for just one more drink, or the urge to engage in another homosexual encounter is often viewed by psychological experts as addictions too powerful to overcome. And yet, Paul declares that no sinful desire is particularly unusual.

A psychotherapist was dealing with a young man in our church who had become involved in homosexuality. As the pastor, I had to confront the young man's sin and call him to immediate repentance if he wanted to continue attending and serving in our fellowship. The psychotherapist scolded me for my insistence that the boy must make an immediate and heart-felt commitment to purity. "It may take some time for him to break off his relationships," the psychotherapist instructed me. "It can take a couple of years."

I turned to the parents who were in the office with us and asked the father, "How long would your wife give you to break off an illicit affair with another woman?" He sheepishly admitted that his wife would insist on an immediate and total turning away from another woman. "So what's the difference?" I asked. Their response indicated that they thought homosexual temptation was categorically different from heterosexual lust. Paul, however, says that there is no temptation that is unique and too strong to resist, if we understand and apply the rest of 1 Corinthians 10:13: **and God is faithful, who will not allow you to be tempted beyond what you are able, but with the temptation will provide the way of escape also, so that you will be able to endure it.**

The Faithfulness of God

Though it is both comforting and helpful to know that your temptations are not unique, that knowledge alone does not provide the power you need to resist. Let's continue to examine Paul's teaching on temptation. **No temptation has overtaken you but such as is common to man; and <u>God is faithful</u> . . . ."**(emphasis mine). I find it encouraging that this thought is not about our ability to resist, but instead, it is about *God's* faithfulness. It means that God is trustworthy and dependable. We can trust His character and His power to enable us to obey His commands. And why, by the way, *does* He give us commands? Is He constantly setting us up to fail so we can experience guilt and unhappiness? Is He looking for opportunities to judge us, to condemn us, and to make us miserable? No, dear ones, our Heavenly Father loves us and wants the very best for us. This is true even in the area of our temptations; God is faithful! That is real hope!

Whereas most psychotherapy teaches the helplessness of victims to overcome their "diseases" without the help of experts and drugs, others swing to the other side of the pendulum and teach that behavioral therapies and strength of self-will can help people overcome their problems. The experts of psychotherapy swing back and forth between the total helplessness of the diseased and the power of human will, but Paul emphasizes God's faithfulness. That is where our hope lies. In His faithfulness, God **will not allow you to be tempted beyond what you are able** (emphasis mine).

When our daughters were teenagers, there were rare moments when they wanted us as parents to make difficult decisions for them. A friend might call asking them to go somewhere or do something that the girls really didn't want to do and knew we would not approve of, but they didn't want to offend their friends. They would look at us with eyes that said, "Please tell me no!" Then they would turn back to the phone and say, "I'm sorry, but my parents won't allow me to go."

It works in a similar way with God—He intervenes for our protection. As a faithful Father, He allows us to wrestle with siblings and play mates, but He will not allow a bully to come and beat us up. Similarly, we must wrestle with our own weaknesses and unrighteous desires, but God will not allow Satan to overwhelm us with temptations that we simply cannot resist. That's a promise! It is an encouraging word that follows, for Paul says, **"you are able."** Note the phrase in this promise: God **will not allow you to be tempted beyond what <u>you are able</u> . . . .** (emphasis mine). We are not helpless victims with no power of choice. God has given us the tools to defeat temptation, if we will only put them to work. The Scriptures define these tools in various passages.

Take for instance James 4:6, where it says that God **gives us more grace,** that is, supernatural power from the Spirit of God to obey His will. There is a condition, however, for Scripture tells us: **"God opposes the proud but gives grace to the humble."** Humility admits, "Lord, I cannot do this on my own. I need your help, your power, and your grace to overcome." Humility submits to God's commands, God's grace, and God's methods, which are so different from the ways of the world. **"For though we live in the world, we do not wage war as the world does"** (2 Corinthians 10:3).

So how do we wage war with the tempter? **Submit yourselves, then, to God. Resist the devil, and he will flee from you** (James 4:7). Note the order: humility of heart, admitting our weakness (v.6), submitting to God by hearing and obeying His Word, and *then* resisting the devil (v.7). You see, we really are able if we will do it God's way.

Paul extends the promise this way in our main passage of 1 Corinthians 10:13: **God is faithful, who will not allow you to be tempted beyond what you are able, but <u>with the temptation</u> will provide the way of escape also, so that you will be able to endure it.** Note that God does not eliminate temptations altogether. We still live in a sin-cursed world, surrounded by unbelievers who are delighted to see us stumble. However, even though we will experience temptation, God will **"provide the way of escape."** How does He do this?

Escape first begins with a "Daniel Decision" (Daniel 1:8). We must choose *beforehand* that we will not put ourselves into situations that guarantee temptation. An "alcoholic," or "drunkard" biblically-speaking, must not go into a bar. One given to sexual sin must not develop friendships with those he is attracted to. One who is drawn by pornography must guard his eyes and avoid the images that lead his heart into sin. If television and computers are too great a temptation, one who wants to please God must avoid them. The writer of Hebrews advises us to **throw off everything that hinders and the sin that so easily entangles and let us run with perseverance the race marked out for us** (Hebrews 12:1).

The second step toward escape is to *prepare* for battle. Paul explains this process fully in Ephesians 6:10-19:

> [10] **Finally, be strong in the Lord and in his mighty power.**
>
> [11] **Put on the full armor of God so that you can take your stand against the devil's schemes.**
>
> [12] **For our struggle is not against flesh and blood, but against the rulers, against the authorities, against the powers of this dark world and against the spiritual forces of evil in the Heavenly realms.**
>
> [13] **Therefore put on the full armor of God, so that when the day of evil comes, you may be able to stand your ground, and after you have done everything, to stand.**
>
> [14] **Stand firm then, with the belt of truth buckled around your waist, with the breastplate of righteousness in place,**
>
> [15] **and with your feet fitted with the readiness that comes from the gospel of peace.**
>
> [16] **In addition to all this, take up the shield of faith, with which you can extinguish all the flaming arrows of the evil one.**
>
> [17] **Take the helmet of salvation and the sword of the Spirit, which is the word of God.**
>
> [18] **And pray in the Spirit on all occasions with all kinds of prayers and requests. With this in mind, be alert and always keep on praying for all the saints.**

Let me take you through a brief tour of spiritual warfare as revealed in the above passage. Verse 10 teaches us that success can only come if we are depending upon the Lord and His power to get us through. If you are confident in yourself, you are toast! Verse 11 says that we must be prepared by fully arming ourselves to overcome our enemy. Verse 12 lets us know whom we are fighting, for we are in a spiritual battle that is extremely difficult, since our enemies are invisible. Verse 13 reminds us that we must do our part in the battle after we have armed ourselves. Verse 14 tells us to hit the battle head on when we have strengthened ourselves with truth and protected ourselves with righteousness. Verse 15 encourages us to take the offensive with the gospel of peace and verse 16 says that we can protect ourselves from temptation with the shield of faith. Verse 17 teaches us to guard our minds with the reality of salvation and to again take the offensive with the Word of God. Verse 18 wraps it all up with the command for continual prayer.

There is full, practical, and powerful teaching in each of those verses, but space does not allow me to detail it for you. This is where your work comes in. Study and meditate on Ephesians 6:10-18 in the context of the battle with temptation. God has given us the tools to escape or overcome the temptations that swirl all around us. If we use weapons He has provided and if we humbly ask for His grace and help, we **will be able to endure it.**

Conclusion

There you have it. Paul has removed all excuses for children of God to continue in defeat by the temptations of the world. God has provided **everything we need for life and godliness through our knowledge of Him** (2 Peter 1:3). God has promised, if we do our part, He will certainly do His in 1 Corinthians 10:13, NASB: **No temptation has overtaken you but such as is common to man; and God is faithful, who will not allow you to be tempted beyond what you are able, but with the temptation will provide the way of escape also, so that you will be able to endure it.**

PERSONAL CONNECTION QUESTIONS

1. Knowing that your own heart is your primary source of temptation, write down three ways you are tempted. Then, write out the root desire behind each one in terms of what you really want (i.e. power, control, pleasure, people to like you, possession of something).

2. Make a "Daniel Decision" for one of the three temptations listed above in Question 1. How can you prepare to battle that temptation? What Scripture verses can you plan to memorize (or write on a 3x5 card) to combat the lies?

Notes

40

Chapter 4
PAUL AND FREEDOM OF THE NEW MAN

Jeff Robinson and Tim Mullet

Did that which is good, then, bring death to me? By
no means! It was sin, producing death in me through
what is good, in order that sin might be shown to be
sin, and through the commandment might become
sinful beyond measure. For we know that the law is
spiritual, but I am of the flesh, sold under sin. For I
do not understand my own actions. For I do not do
what I want, but I do the very thing I hate. Now if
I do what I do not want, I agree with the law, that
it is good. So now it is no longer I who do it, but
sin that dwells within me. For I know that nothing
good dwells in me, that is, in my flesh. For I have the
desire to do what is right, but not the ability to carry
it out. For I do not do the good I want, but the evil
I do not want is what I keep on doing. Now if I do
what I do not want, it is no longer I who do it, but sin
that dwells within me.

So I find it to be a law that when I want to do right,
evil lies close at hand. For I delight in the law of
God, in my inner being, but I see in my members
another law waging war against the law of my mind
and making me captive to the law of sin that dwells
in my members. Wretched man that I am! Who will
deliver me from this body of death? Thanks be to
God through Jesus Christ our Lord! So then, I myself
serve the law of God with my mind, but with my
flesh I serve the law of sin.
                    Romans 7:13-25

Struggling with Sin?

It is easy in our therapeutic society to speak of our struggles. A
person who has cancer for years is triumphantly described as
struggling with cancer. In a similar way, a person who has abused his

family through years of alcoholic consumption is, in some cases, no less triumphantly described as having struggled with "alcoholism" for years. When a person comes to you for counseling and you ask them why they have come, typically their problem is worded in the language of struggle. "I have come because I struggle with loneliness, dissatisfaction, bitterness, depression, etc."

There is no shortage of circumstances with which to struggle, seemingly less shortage of strugglers and at a certain point, one begins to wonder what exactly this word struggle means. How is it being used? Why is it appropriate to speak of one's struggle with cancer and at the same time speak of struggling with headaches or bad hair? Do all inconveniences merit the language of struggle? Isn't there a difference between struggle and resignation? Doesn't the word actually signify an active form of combat? These are the sorts of impolite questions one may begin to ask in a society where many are said to be struggling and few are said to be holy. And make no mistake; there is little that is seen as more rude or intolerant than to question the legitimacy of someone's experience. If a person thinks himself to be struggling, then who are you to call into question their experience? Yet the simple fact remains that we are all struggling with something.

In many ways this slippery understanding of struggling has infiltrated our understanding of the believer's relationship to sin. A believer's relationship to sin is said to be a struggle with sin, and so a believer is said to struggle with anger, pornography, fulfillment, anxiety, etc. For example, consider the husband who is said to struggle with road rage or the wife who struggles with homemaking. At the very least we ought to ask about the nature of these struggles. If you angrily honk the horn whenever someone is not driving at a speed you think appropriate, in what sense is this actually a struggle with road rage? In a similar way, should struggling with homemaking result in a sustained pattern of laziness and idleness followed by depression? Of course, we know that life is not this simple and neither are people.

Struggle is a thing of degree, and people are rarely so easily caricatured, and yet the question remains. Should a habitual and sustained pattern of sin be appropriately deemed a struggle with sin? In many cases we use the word "struggle" in exactly this sense, describing a person who perceives himself, whether legitimately or illegitimately, to be suffering from any sort of affliction, irrespective of the absence of sustained resistance. To struggle is to suffer. Yet, one would be hard pressed to find this novel understanding of struggling in the Scriptures. As a result, our point in all of this is to gain a sense of clarity as to the nature of biblical struggling.

The Bible clearly describes the Christian life as a struggle with sin. It is our conviction that Paul, in Romans 7, speaks of his own personal struggle with sin as a believer. We do not see this as the struggle of a non-believer.[8] However, the Christian's struggle with sin is very different than the current psychological struggles with perceived afflictions. In order to struggle with sin, one must fight sin, resist sin, and wage war against sin. Therefore, when we speak of struggling with sin, we will be speaking of the Christian's war against sin. In this respect, the Christian has been set free to struggle.

Paul's Own Experience of Struggling

The Scriptures present the Apostle Paul as a positive example for us to follow in the Christian life. Paul himself would say as much, exhorting us to imitate him as he imitates Christ (1 Corinthians 11:1). As a result, when we read the Scriptures, we may be tempted to think of people like Paul as belonging to some category of Christian experience that is entirely different from our own.

Intellectually we know that Paul is not Jesus and is therefore still a sinner in need of grace. And certainly we remember Paul's great experience of grace on the Damascus Road; which is given much space in Acts and Galatians. Yet, it is often difficult to think of the continual daily grace that Paul needed to actually live the Christian life. It is much easier to think of Paul as the former terrorist turned missionary who evangelized the known world, rather than the fellow struggler who hated and despised his own sinfulness, a struggler who

---

8   The question of whether Paul is speaking in Romans 7 as a believer or as a "pre-believer" is the subject of debate among contemporary evangelical scholars. Reformed theologians tend to view this text as depicting Paul the believer wrangling with indwelling sin. Non-Reformed theologians tend to view Romans 7 as Paul's biographical account of his struggle with sin before submitting to Christ as Lord and Savior. John Calvin himself viewed Romans 7 as the struggles of Paul, the Christ-follower. Not all Reformed theologians agree with his assessment and not all non-Reformed theologians take this chapter as the self-analysis of Paul, the unbeliever.

reminded himself daily of his freedom from condemnation (Romans 8:1). As a result, it can be comforting for the believer to hear Paul confess, **"I do not understand my own actions. For I do not do what I want, but I do the very thing I hate"** (Romans 7:15).

It can be comforting to know that Paul was indeed a fellow struggler instead of the idealized sinless version that we might be tempted to imagine. The more we see Paul as a real human being, the less we will despair and the more we will begin to see how Paul's counsel can actually help us in our struggle with sin, instead of placing before us an insurmountable obstacle of piety. For this reason, Paul provides for us a better example of the process of sanctification in the Christian life by pointing us to Jesus Christ Himself. A sinless person does indeed set the standard for how to live, but does not provide an example of what daily repentance looks like.

How Paul's Example Helps Us

1. In order to struggle with sin we must hate sin.

The first thing of note in looking to Paul for help in struggling with sin is a deep hatred for sin. It is hard to imagine the words **"wretched man that I am"** (Romans 7:24) coming from someone who thinks little of the importance of fighting sin. Yet, if there is anything that characterizes the contemporary church it is an unwillingness to speak about sin. At best, the church harbors very shallow thoughts about the grievous nature of sin. Wherever the true church manifests itself you will find a deep and abiding hatred for sin and a longing for holiness. As such, there is no sense in which a Christian may be truly said to be struggling with a sin that he does not hate. Hatred for sin is a pre-requisite for our struggle with sin. Unless we begin to hate the sin that we see in our lives, in solidarity with Paul, **"I do the very thing I hate"** (Romans 7:15), we will never actually struggle with sin. This principle is true in general and also true in terms of "pet" sins or "respectable" sins. Often we see very little progress in our lives in areas such as gossip, complaining, and anger, because while we may be the first to admit that these sins are objectively wrong, we do not hate them.

2. In order to struggle with sin we must understand sin's bondage.

Anyone who has struggled with sin knows something of sin's bondage. There is nothing more characteristic of a lost person than his bondage to sin. The unbeliever is so characterized by his sinfulness that the Apostle would describe all unbelievers as being slaves of sin (Romans 6:17), who presented *their* members as slaves to impurity and lawlessness leading to more lawlessness (Romans 6:19). To be a slave of sin is to be owned by sin. Contrary to what you may think, before becoming a Christian you do not in fact belong to yourself. Your will is bound by sin and you are powerless to resist it. The more a person transgresses, the easier sin becomes, the more normal that it seems and the more difficult it is to turn from sin. Lawlessness leads to more lawlessness. There is no such thing as an individual who struggles with one sin; his sin is connected to many other sins in ways he probably does not even realize.

The more an individual begins to fight specific sins the more he realizes how comprehensive his problems truly are. Yet, no victory is possible until a person is saved, and salvation cannot come to a person until he sees his inability to live a righteous life in his own strength. Indeed it is difficult to imagine the existence of a Christian who understands nothing of the enslaving power of sin. It is the tax collectors, the harlots, and the Gentiles who find mercy, and it is quite clear that unless you see yourself as poor, blind, wretched and miserable you will not be saved. Those who are well have no need of a physician, and yet none are well and few see their need of The Physician. Sin is binding. As a result, in order to struggle with sin, we must come to see the binding nature of sin, and how powerless we are to fight sin in our own strength.

3. In order to struggle with sin we must understand the relationship between sin and affliction.

To sin is to suffer. However, the great deception lies in the source of our suffering. It is not uncommon for a wife who struggles with depression to fail to see the connection between her suffering (depression) and her sin (laziness in homemaking). The same is true for a husband who struggles with road rage. More often than not it is the other drivers who are identified as the source of his suffering instead of an angry and impatient heart. Jesus Christ died to save sinners from their sin, and it is those who see their sin and despise it most deeply who fall on their faces seeking mercy. Salvation cannot come to a man who does not understand his bondage to sin, neither will it come to a man who cannot see the connection between his own sinfulness and the affliction he suffers. As a result, the problem is not that many want to rid themselves of affliction, the problem is that they *only* want to rid themselves of affliction and do not want to rid themselves of the source of their affliction. Thus, when we look to Paul we see a person who sees sin for the plague that it is and has cultivated a deep and abiding hatred for it and the bondage that results from it.

4. In order to struggle with sin we must understand Christian liberty.

Paul also helps us to struggle with sin by giving us a right understanding of Christian liberty. Christ's coming is sometimes viewed as returning everyone to a state in which everyone is free to do what is right in their own eyes. The problem with this understanding of Christian liberty is that it fails to understand that **the law is holy, and the commandment is holy and righteous and good** (Romans 7:12). Anarchy is never seen as a better replacement for law. If holiness is the goal, then one must have an objective standard by which to measure the actual progression towards holiness. In doing away with law, one also does away with holiness. For Paul, lawlessness is the enemy, not the goal.

As sinners, however, we are tempted to think of the law entirely in negative terms. Inherent to our fallenness is a mistrust of laws and lawgivers. As a result, Satan's assault on God's moral law in the garden was an assault on the character of God. Why would this God be needlessly restrictive or oppressive? Why would this God restrict what is good? Only an evil tyrant would withhold good from His creatures. It is good to be like God; therefore, you should not trust this jealous God who zealously seeks to guard his own power. Satan operates in much the same way today. Prohibitions are seen to be evil, even if those prohibitions are restrictions from evil. To be a sinner is to do what is right in your own eyes. Unfortunately, this is an entirely subjective experience; what is right to one is wrong to another. Thus, sinners are in need of an objective moral standard.

Fortunately, God has not left us to our own subjective moral determinations and has graciously given us objective, revealed moral laws. Certainly these laws are given progressively to God's people throughout history in various administrations and are summarized in the Ten Commandments of Exodus 20. Yet, to the sinner, these laws, whatever the administration, are seen to be restrictive or oppressive. Part of this oppression is experienced as a result of a law's confrontation of our own sinful desires. God's law says "no" to that which my wicked heart says "yes." For this reason God's law feels oppressive. The law can also be oppressive to the sinner in another sense. This law says no to what my convicted heart agrees with and yet my will is powerless to turn from. Either way, to the sinner the law can only be experienced as a form of oppression; yet, Paul told Timothy, **Now we know that the law is good, if one uses it lawfully, understanding this that the law is not laid down for the just, but for the lawless and disobedient, for the ungodly and the sinners . . . .** (1 Timothy 1:8-9a). The law is not oppressive, but is God's mechanism that exposes the wickedness of the human heart and drives the sinner to seek forgiveness and reconciliation in the Savior. The law is good because it is also restrictive, in the manner of a godly parent setting good and necessary boundaries for a child.

In order to illustrate this point, Paul invites us to consider the nature of marriage. Marriage is certainly a type of bondage in that it restricts freedom. A husband is no longer free to predominantly pursue self-interest or even the interests of Christ, but his cares are divided (1 Corinthians 7:1). A happily married man would see this restriction of freedom in a positive light; he delights in pleasing his spouse and the good gifts of marriage. As a result, the bondage of marriage is not seen as burdensome to him. On the other hand the unhappily married man might consider the corner of a rooftop a better abode than to dwell with the wife to whom he is bound. His bondage is a burden. As a result, to say that a man is bound to the law or bound to a wife is simply to say that in either case his freedom is restricted. A married man does not have the same freedom as a single man; he has obligations to his wife. He has made commitments to her and her alone. In a similar respect, the unbeliever is not freed to do all that his carnal mind may wish. The law restricts his freedom and serves to condemn his unrighteous acts.

In either case, death brings about liberty. If a woman's husband dies, she is free to remarry (Romans 7:2). His death releases her from the bondage of the marriage covenant and she is free to marry another. If the unbeliever dies and is born anew, he also experiences a change of obligation. His primary obligation is no longer to the law, but to Christ. He *has* died to the law through the body of Christ, so that *he* may belong to another (Romans 7:4). In this sense, the law is binding on a person only as long as he lives. The law declares a murderer to be a murderer for the duration of his life. In many places, the penalty for murder is death. As a result, as long as the murderer lives, the law serves to condemn him as guilty. There is no way to balance the scales or give back the life he took; he is guilty. When he dies, however, the law has no more power to condemn him. He has paid for his crime.

Therefore, salvation fundamentally changes the sinner's experience of law. What once served to entice and condemn us now can be seen for the good that it was originally intended. Jesus' death and resurrection serves as a paradigm for our own experience of salvation. To be a Christian is to die a death like His in order that we might be raised to walk in newness of life. God's law, which is a gracious reflection of His character, no longer retains its condemning power. There is therefore no condemnation for those who are in Christ Jesus (Romans 8:1). Yet, we are set free not only from the penalty of sin, but also the power of sin. To be a Christian is to have the power of sin broken in our lives so that instead of being slaves of sin, we become slaves of righteousness (Romans 6:18). The purpose of our freedom is so that we might actually bear fruit for God (Romans 7:4). As a result, the doctrine of Christian liberty is of essential importance to counseling believers. If we do not understand the Christian's relationship to the law we will make no progress in our struggle against sin, because to be a Christian is to be set free to struggle.

The Struggle between the Flesh and the Spirit

If the good news sets us free from the power of sin, so that we are no longer slaves of sin, why is it that we still sin? When you emancipate a slave, the slave does not automatically possess the habits of a free man, but the habits of a slave. Legally, he is declared to be free and no longer under the ownership of his master, but functionally it might take time to adjust. The same thing is true of the Christian. While we are legally emancipated from the slavery of sin, we have the habits of a slave. As a result, the Christian life involves a struggle to realize one's new identity. You are no longer a slave but free. You no longer have to set your mind on the things of the flesh but the Spirit. The law no longer has to condemn us but can be fulfilled by us through the indwelling Spirit of God.

One of the major problems that sensitive Christians face when attempting to live the Christian life is unrealistic expectations. The Christian life is a life of struggle, not ease. If it took you twenty years to get into a particular sinful pattern of life, it might take you twenty years to get out of it. This is no reflection of the ability of Christ to instantaneously deliver you from your sin, but a reflection on the comprehensive nature of sin. Lawlessness leads to more lawlessness. One sin is connected to other sins. A person who struggles with anger might also struggle with complaining, irritability, pride, joy, the temptation to find fulfillment in work, busyness, etc. In the same way a person who struggles with laziness might also struggle with contentment, joy, body image, purpose, discipline, and frustration. When one takes a sobering look at his life and the comprehensive nature of his problems, there is only one appropriate response: "Who will deliver me from this body of death?" Yet we must keep in mind that it is God's grace that allows us to hate the sin that we see in our lives and it is only by that same grace that we will make any progress in fighting specific sins. The best advice we can give is to start somewhere. The more that you begin to see victory in one area of your life, the more you will see other strongholds falling.

The Eschaton and the End of Struggle

Finally, we must understand as we struggle with sin, that our struggle is limited to this present age. There is little more encouraging to the soldier than to know that the end of the war is near. The Christian life is not a sprint but a marathon, and sometimes we become weary. Certainly there is little more discouraging than to know that you are fighting a battle that will never end, but this is not the case with the Christian. It is true that our battle will last the duration of our lives, but there is an end to our struggle. We are saved in the hope that one day the fight will be over. One day we will be completely free of all remnant sin. Our bodies will no longer be decaying but glorified. The struggle will be over. We are not fighting a losing battle but a winning battle. What God started, he will finish. He has set us free from the power of sin so that we might be progressively conformed to the image of His Son. While we cannot trust our willpower, we can trust Him to finish the work He started.

How Now Shall We Live? John Owen and the Mortification of Sin in Believers

John Owen (1616-1683) was deservedly called "the prince among Puritans" for his massive intellect and prodigious ability to crank out works of theology and practical divinity (his works are 16 volumes, plus Hebrews, and a Biblical Theology, among others). He was sent to Oxford University at the age of 12, where he studied for 10 years and was such an intense scholar, he allowed himself only four hours of sleep per night. He pastored for many years in congregational churches in London, including a 2000-member church from 1646-1652. In 1652, Owen was appointed vice-chancellor at Oxford and later wrote a tremendously influential confession of faith for Congregationalists based on the Westminster Confession of Faith called *The Savoy Declaration*. Among his works are books on the Holy Spirit, Communion with God, apostasy from the Gospel, and the glory of Christ. Difficult to read in places, his clearest and best-known work today is called *On the Mortification of Sin in Believers*. He also served as chaplain in Cromwell's army.

Putting sin on the gallows is the crux of *On the Mortification of Sin in Believers*. This work and this man are so important for counselors and pastors today because it is crucial for us to get the doctrine of human nature right before we can give the right diagnosis to cure man's "sickness" rightly called "sin." Scripture tells us that sin is that deadly disease and that grace is the cure. Owen helps us to diagnose the cancer and provides its cure in this excellent meditation and application of Romans 8:13: **For if you live according to the flesh you will die, but if by the Spirit you put to death the deeds of the body, you will live.**

An outline of the second chapter alone provides excellent counsel to all believers in all ages. After defining the mortification of sin carefully as the *intentional*, daily task of the putting to death of indwelling sin, Owen argues that all Christians ought to make the mortification of indwelling sin their daily work because:

- Indwelling sin always abides, therefore it must always be mortified.
- Indwelling sin not only abides, but is still acting.
- Indwelling sin is not only active, but will produce soul-destroying sins if not mortified. Here, he directs readers to the catalog of sins in Galatians 5:19-21 that will inevitably arise if the heart is not purified daily through the killing of sin: **adultery, fornication, uncleanness, lust, idolatry, witchcraft, hatred, jealousy, wrath, strife, seditions, heresies, envy, murder, drunkenness . . . .**
- Indwelling sin is to be opposed by the Spirit and the new nature.

And what is the result of neglecting the mortification of sin in the believer? John Owen states, "Where sin, through the neglect of mortification, gets a considerable victory, it breaks the bones of the soul (Psalm 31:10; 51:8), and makes a man weak, sick, and ready to die (Psalm 38:3-5), so that he cannot look up (Psalm 40:12; Isaiah 33:24); and when poor creatures will take blow after blow, wound after wound, foil after foil, and never rouse up themselves to a vigorous opposition, can they expect anything but to be hardened through the deceitfulness of sin, and that their souls should bleed to death." Christians, including all biblical counselors, cannot afford to neglect sin in their personal lives, the lives of those they offer counsel, nor the family of faith. Freedom awaits those who are honest, diligent, and brutal toward the sin in their own lives.

PERSONAL CONNECTION QUESTIONS

1. How sensitive are you to the sinful attitudes and desires in your own heart that tempt you to trust yourself rather than Christ (Proverbs 3:5-8)? Ask someone very close to you to identify three to five sinful habit patterns that they are aware you struggle with. Then, devise a list of put-on thoughts, words, and behaviors with which to replace the sinful ones.

2. How honest are you with others about their sinful words and actions? Are you bold in confronting them with sin? Are you gentle when you do so, acknowledging your own sin first (Matthew 7:3-5)? Ask someone very close to you for feedback about how you sound and look when you point out their sin. Work on balancing truth and grace in your life when you confront the sin in others (John 1:14; Ephesians 4:15-16).

Chapter 5
PAUL AND FREEDOM: WALK BY THE SPIRIT

Tim Keeter and Fred J. Bucci

> **For you were called to freedom, brothers. Only do not use your freedom as an opportunity for the flesh, but through love serve one another. For the whole law is fulfilled in one word: "You shall love your neighbor as yourself." But if you bite and devour one another, watch out that you are not consumed by one another. But I say, walk by the Spirit, and you will not gratify the desires of the flesh. For the desires of the flesh are against the Spirit, and the desires of the Spirit are against the flesh, for these are opposed to each other, to keep you from doing the things you want to do. But if you are led by the Spirit, you are not under the law.**
>
> Galatians 5:13-18

Have you ever come to what is called a "fork in the road"? This is typically the place where you must make a decision to go right or left. For the follower of Christ, this dilemma is a stark reality faced quite regularly, and sometimes even moment by moment. The choice for the Christian involves "walking" down one of two paths, described in the Galatians passage above. One path leads to "self-glory" and is called the flesh, while the other path leads to glorifying God and is called walking in the Spirit.

As believers in Christ, our "walk" is how we "live out" our lives. The problem we face is that we are well-practiced at living according to our sinful desires; so much so that it often seems to take little or no effort at all to pursue and fulfill the desires of our flesh. This compounds sin's deceptiveness as we can easily travel far down this path and strengthen sinful habits, unaware of our offense before a holy God.

On the other hand, we see that Scripture calls us to walk the other path; to "walk by the Spirit." This phrase can seem like a nice collection of Christian words to sweetly describe a nearly impossible task, but Paul makes it very clear to the Galatians, and to us, that walking in the Spirit is exactly the remedy for putting to death those sinful desires of the flesh. And throughout all of his epistles, Paul tells us how to do it.

What "Walking in the Spirit" Means

Our first concern is to really understand what is meant by walking "in" or "by" the flesh or the Spirit. In the New Testament, to do something in the Spirit means to depend upon the ministry of the Holy Spirit in order to accomplish genuine obedience. Likewise, walking in the flesh indicates that we are depending on ourselves, in our flesh, to accomplish genuine obedience: a state of mind that is self-centered, full of spiritual pride, and tainted with legalism. And, as we'll see later, that's putting it lightly.

What directs our walk? It is whatever we set our minds (hearts, desires, treasures, motives, thoughts) upon. Paul understood, and wanted the Galatians to understand, that people continually live for whatever they have set their hearts to pursue and obtain. So if we set our heart to pursue that which the Spirit wills us to pursue, then we are walking by the Spirit. Set your heart upon self-centered, idolatrous cravings, and you will certainly walk in the flesh. The two mutually oppose one another, making it even more pressing that we understand this clearly. Notice how clearly Paul summarizes this truth for the Roman believers:

> **For those who live according to the flesh set their minds on the things of the flesh, but those who live according to the Spirit set their minds on the things of the Spirit** (Romans 8:5).

In counseling, we recognize that if we want to discern what our counselees have inwardly set their hearts to pursue, we (together with them) have to observe the outward evidence of those pursuits in their speech and behavior (Luke 6:45; Matthew 15:18-19). Paul wanted to make sure that the Galatians clearly knew when they were walking in the flesh. He did this by describing the "deeds of the flesh" in Galatians 5:19-21 that they could expect to (and indeed did) see in their lives. We can see how persistence in fleshly pursuits plays out in the ugliest of ways, even for believers. Paul lists sins of sexual depravity (immorality, impurity, sensuality), sins of religion (idolatry, sorcery), social sins that affect our human relationships (enmities, strife, jealousy, outbursts of anger, disputes, dissentions, factions, envying), and sins dealing with alcohol (drunkenness, carousing) as **"works of the flesh."** This list is far from exhaustive, and worse, habitual continuation of these is characteristic of unbelievers, a shameful thing for a redeemed child of God to imitate.

When we are controlled by our selfish desires, we are deceived, and our sinful indulgence can come across in some very subtle ways that may even masquerade as righteous. (Example: Engaging in ministry in order to attract the praise, approval, and adoration of others instead of from God.)

Deeds of the Flesh: Digging Deeper

Let's dig a little deeper with Paul into what's behind these deeds of the flesh for the believer beginning with Galatians 5:13: **For you were called to freedom, brethren; only do not turn your freedom into an opportunity for the flesh** (NASB). Freedom. As children of God, our sins have been paid in full, so from the moment of our salvation, there is **no condemnation** whatsoever because it was all laid upon our Savior (Romans 8:1). We are therefore free from the curse of the law because Christ became **a curse for us** (Galatians 3:13). God's purpose for the Law that He provided through Moses in the Old Testament is and always has been to **become our tutor to lead us to Christ, so that we may be justified by faith** (Galatians 3:24). How does the Law do that? It functions to identify sin, pronounce our guilt and full responsibility for our sin, and conclude without question that we are fully deserving of God's judgment. That's all the law can do; it cannot produce the fruit of the Spirit, prevent us from sinning, or reconcile us in peace with God. Its purpose is to boldly reveal to us that we cannot keep the law faithfully and God's intention then is to draw us to repentance, confessing Christ as Lord.

And so we rightly celebrate that **by grace you have been saved through faith; and that not of yourselves, it is the gift of God; not as a result of works, so that no one may boast** (Ephesians 2:8–9). No Bible-believing Christian would claim otherwise; we would never dare to take credit for our own salvation by adding our own works to Christ's. We proclaim that we are saved by faith alone—and nothing we have done or will ever do can change that. Likewise, when we are saved, our relationship to the law changes in that it becomes a delight and joy to us (Romans 7:22; Psalm 1:2; 119:47). Are we doing a good enough job challenging our counselees with this point? Why then do we turn to our selfish desires and live apart from dependence on the Holy Spirit? The ultimate penalty for sin has been removed, and so this rebellion that still resides within us foolishly seeks to take advantage of that freedom (from the curse of the law and the slavery of sin). Thus, our outward actions become a poor substitute for the inward holiness we are called to pursue.

But sadly, that's the deception of sin and its fleeting rewards, because it never delivers what it promises. We can see how that has been played out in the narrative of our lives. Before salvation, we were under bondage to the law. When we live by the flesh, we place ourselves right back under bondage for as long as we persist in our sin. We could state the converse of verse 18 like this: "If you are not led by the Spirit, you are under the Law."

This is the essence of legalism: choosing your works as the principle by which you relate to God. Paul isn't making a case against good works, but stating that when we fall into legalism, we lose our grip on grace.

How can we tell when we have fallen into legalism? We find ourselves under bondage when obedience becomes a duty, a drudgery, and oppressive because we can't do it all perfectly—and so we become estranged from Christ until we repent. For this, the Galatians earned a stern, fatherly rebuke from Paul. We and our counselees should take this to heart as well because God does not want us to be legalistic by thinking we can earn God's favor.

When we walk in the flesh, we should note an intense inner conflict within us. **For the flesh sets its desire against the Spirit, and the Spirit against the flesh; for these are in opposition to one another, so that you may not do the things that you please** (Galatians 5:17; NASB). Only God rules the hearts of believers, but sin can push us and force itself upon us because we still must choose to submit to God's Word. Sin is persistent and present, even when we are at our best (Romans 7:21). Our fleshly desires never rest, constantly opposing our godly desires and actions. There is a war inside of us.

Therefore, when we choose to submit to the inner desires of the flesh, this sin within only serves to intensify the inner conflict and your conscience works to bring you to realize your need of repentance.

It was for freedom that Christ set us free; therefore keep standing firm and do not be subject again to a yoke of slavery (Galatians 5:1; NASB). Repentance is to be a daily way of life for the believer. Turning from self-indulgent desires of the flesh toward the likeness of Christ is an evidence of God's grace. Our ever-maturing desire and ability to become more like Christ is begun and sustained in us by the Holy Spirit.

So then how do we "walk in the Spirit"? Is walking in the Spirit passive on our part so that we just sit and wait for it to happen? Or is it something that we do alone apart from God? It is neither! Walking in the Spirit is part of the Holy Spirit's ministry in the life of every believer as He commands our obedience and joyful cooperation. The very word "walk" implies action and we are to partner with God's Spirit. Let's look at what walking by the Spirit produces first and then conclude with how to cultivate it in our lives and the lives of those to whom we minister.

A Fruitful Walk

In stark contrast to the deeds of the flesh, Paul lists the deeds (**"fruit"**) of the Spirit. These are a natural byproduct of the Holy Spirit working in us and thus never a thing for which we can take an ounce of credit.

Love	Do you love your neighbor, especially those in your church family? **"By this all men will know that you are My disciples, if you have love for one another"** (John 13:35).
Joy	Is your joy ever present? Unlike happiness in a secular sense, biblical joy is independent of our circumstances because it is rooted in the Lord (Philippians 4:4).

Peace	This is peace *with* God, which is entirely His gift to us through Jesus Christ. Are you at peace with Him or do you think of yourself as an enemy (Romans 5:1-2; James 4:4)?
Patience	Do you put up well with others, even when severely tried for a lengthy period of time?
Kindness	Is your kindness towards others reflective of God's kindness toward you?
Goodness	Are you actively generous toward others, even when it's unmerited?
Faithfulness	Are you known as trustworthy and reliable?
Gentleness	Are you so much in control that you are angry at the right time and not angry at the wrong time?
Self-control	Do you regularly experience inward and outward triumph over fleshly desires (walking in the world without being influenced by it)?

Brothers and sisters in Christ, don't be discouraged by this list—this is God's commitment to complete what He began in you through the power of the Holy Spirit, if you truly belong to Him (Philippians1:6)! Maturity in these characteristics is an ongoing, progressive process, and as you persist in them (by grace!), then you will at the same time be gradually subduing the flesh. **But I say, walk by the Spirit, and you will not carry out the desire of the flesh** (Galatians 5:16).

Just as in our salvation, it is the Spirit *alone* who keeps the believer truly free. We can therefore expect our sinful habits to stop returning over and over again with the same intensity if we are repenting[9] and walking in the Spirit. Upon salvation, the old habits and nature of sin are not eradicated, but they become increasingly subdued in the life of every believer who learns by grace to walk

---

9   Grudem, Wayne, *Systemic Theology*, (Grand Rapids, Zondervan Publishers, 1994).Repentance should not be confused with confession. *Repentance is a heartfelt sorrow for sin, a renouncing of it, and a sincere commitment to forsake it and walk in obedience to Christ.*

in the Spirit. We must still necessarily and consciously choose to go God's way—and to do so with full dependence on Him. There is simply no other way.

Dr. Wayne Grudem clarifys how we are to walk in the Holy Spirit. The Holy Spirit is God's presence manifest within every believer. He writes that "in the Holy Spirit" means "that we consciously dwell in the . . . sense of the presence of the Holy Spirit himself." There are many New Testament examples of how we live and act "in the Spirit." Here are a few:

- **Rejoice greatly in the Holy Spirit** (Luke 10:21)
- **Paul purposed** [decided to do something] **in the Spirit** (Acts 19:21)
- **Paul's conscience testifies with me in the Holy Spirit** (Romans 9:1)
- **Through Him we both have our access in one Spirit to the Father** (Ephesians 2:18)
- **Pray at all times in the Spirit** (Ephesians 6:18)
- **Love in the Spirit** (Colossians 1:8)

What distinguishes loving in the Spirit from simply loving? To do something "in the Spirit" means you make a conscious and deliberate effort to prayerfully remember that you depend on the ministry and power of the Holy Spirit within you to do something that pleases God and fulfills your calling as His child. When you love, your desire is to see God glorified in the response of the person being loved. Self-adulation fades away when your primary desire is for the love of Christ to be experienced in others. The apostle Paul wanted Christians to know that when they love God and love others, they can only do so genuinely when they remember it is God's grace that enables them to do so. The principle of dependence on the Spirit wonderfully opposes our self-centeredness and dependence on self to accomplish genuine obedience.

This is admittedly not natural to us. We are incapable of "agape," or unconditional love, apart from Christ. Here is a list of principles intended to help cultivate maturity in this area:

1. Continually regard the flesh as crucified (Galatians 3:20). Take hope in Philippians 1:6; God is far more committed to conforming us to Christ than we are willing to enjoy the passing pleasures of sin. Within us is a warrior infinitely determined and committed to the destruction of the flesh.

2. Guard and increase the spiritual disciplines of Bible intake (reading, listening, meditation, and memorization) and private biblical prayer.

3. Biblical thinking: Don't live your life passively. Consciously remind yourself of your dependence on the Spirit and God's grace in your prayers, thoughts, and actions. This opposes living hour by hour as if God already did everything He was going to do for you at salvation or that He's merely standing by in case you need Him for something.

4. Biblical service: Seek to glorify Christ by serving one another in love, actively engaged in the "one anothers" of Scripture with a local church family and your community.

5. Biblical humility: Be transparent with those who are close to you, and guard against living for yourself or for the esteem of others.

Counseling Application

Walking in the Spirit is an ongoing struggle because the war between the Spirit and the flesh is a raging battle. The flesh is constantly setting its desire against the Spirit of God that dwells in every believer's heart (Galatians 5:17 NASB). The flesh is best described as the enemy within us. Romans 7:18 (NASB) states that **"nothing good dwells in me, that is, in my flesh."** Romans 7:21 (NASB) goes on to clarify that the flesh is sinful and an **"evil that is present in me."**

Many times Christians who struggle with their flesh feel hopeless and helpless in this war. They look at Galatians 5:16 (NASB) where it states, **"Walk in the Spirit and you will not carry out the desire of the flesh"** and say, "It is not working for me." The obvious next step is to ask them to describe their idea of walking in the Spirit. Some typical responses would include reading the Bible, going to church, going to a small group Bible study, and other ministry involvement. These are very good disciplines, but some may reveal a lesser involvement in religious disciplines. There may be a 'disconnect' from these activities because of heart motives. If we are not powered by the Holy Spirit and motivated by His perfect love, then those worthy activities are reduced to fleshly works.

Why is it that the counselee is struggling with putting off the old man and putting on the new man as described in Ephesians 4:22-24 and Colossians 3:8-10 (NASB)? As biblical counselors, we are called as agents of God's Holy Spirit (2 Timothy 2:20-21, NASB) to determine why the counselee is not able to make the connection between knowing what is right to do and being able to do it from a heart devoted to Him (James 4:17, NASB). As biblical counselors, we realize it is the Holy Spirit who illuminates the inner man to sanctification (Ephesians 4:16; NASB), and is warring on our behalf in the sanctification process (Galatians 5:17; NASB). The Holy Spirit is active in multiple ways by working on the hearts of Christians who struggle to overcome the flesh (Philippians 2:13; NASB). God's holy and written Word informs our minds with absolute truth and judges our hearts' intentions (2 Timothy 3:16-17; Hebrews 4:12; 1 Thessalonians 2:13 NASB).

Jesus stated that He would not leave us as orphans but would give us the **"Spirit of Truth"** who will **"abide with you and be in you"** (John 14:17; NASB). The Holy Spirit is called the "Helper" whom the Father will send (John 14:26 NASB). So again, why the 'disconnect' in understanding the Word of God and not doing what it says to do? Many counselees mistakenly take a mystical view of how the Holy Spirit works in them by expecting God to do all of the work. In other words, they think that if the Spirit is warring against the flesh as Galatians 5:17 (NASB) says, then it is God's responsibility to cause them not to sin. Their practical understanding is that God will do the work for them, and if they don't succeed, it is God's fault. But they are missing the idea behind Philippians 2:12-13 (NASB). These verses clearly state that we are to **"work out our salvation in fear and trembling"** while it is **"God who is at work in you both to will and to work for His good pleasure."** There is this dynamic of God working together with us in the process of warring against the flesh and putting off the old man and putting on the new man. I believe the disconnect between knowing and doing God's Word is the result of Christians not taking up their spiritual weapons and armor for the battle (Ephesians 6:10-18, NASB).

At this point in a counseling discussion, I usually point to Romans 8:12-13 (NASB) to show counselees that they are no longer under obligation to their flesh and they must **"put to death the deeds of the body."** This is referred to by John Owen as 'mortifying the flesh.' Some have referred to this active warfare against the flesh as becoming violent for the kingdom of God (Matthew 11:12 NASB). When struggling people realize their responsibility in the battle of the flesh and the Spirit, there seems to be some improvement in their transformation into Christ's character (Romans 8:29 NASB).

John Owen states in *The Mortification of Sin* on page 46: "He doth not so work our mortification in us as not to keep it still an act of our obedience. The Holy Ghost works in us and upon us, as we are fit to be wrought in and upon; that is, so as to preserve our own liberty and free obedience. He works upon our understandings, wills, consciences and affections, agreeably to their own natures: He works in us and with us, not against us or without us: so that His assistance is an encouragement as to the facilitating of the work, and no occasion of neglect as to the work itself." I believe John Owen truly grasps the idea of how we and God interact in the process of mortifying the flesh and walking in the Spirit. When this is understood, the mysterious partnership is very helpful in the counseling room.

Conclusion

The war inside is very real for the Christian, yet it is not as mystical as some are led to believe. It is spiritual but not mystical. By God's grace, the believer in Christ can learn to say "no" to the fleshly desires within and say "yes" to the Holy Spirit's power to transform. The choice whether to walk in the Spirit or in the flesh is squarely placed upon each person by God's design. Each person is responsible for every choice in thought, word, and deed. In God's wisdom, He uses His Word working in partnership with the Holy Spirit to empower and embolden the follower of Christ to make choices that deny the flesh and ultimately glorify Him.

PERSONAL CONNECTION QUESTIONS

1.   Like the psalmist in Psalm 139:23-24, pray this prayer aloud now: **"Search me, O God, and know my heart; try me and know my anxious thoughts; and see if there be any hurtful way in me, And lead me in the everlasting way."** Find other prayers from the Bible to pray that acknowledge your great need for Christ even as a believer in Him.

2. Make a list of the good deeds you have done in the past two weeks. What was your heart motive behind each good deed? Were you seeking some form of gain that would help you personally? Were you doing something for someone else purely for no other reason than to glorify God?

3. Find a person you can serve who can do nothing in return to "pay you back." Serve them and when they thank you, give the glory to God alone.

Notes

Chapter 6
PAUL AND THINKING:
RENEWING THE MIND

Andy Wisner and Tim Mullet

I appeal to you therefore, brothers, by the mercies of God, to present your bodies as a living sacrifice, holy and acceptable to God, which is your spiritual worship. Do not be conformed to this world, but be transformed by the renewal of your mind, that by testing you may discern what is the will of God, what is good and acceptable and perfect.
Romans 12:1-2

How can it be that I want conflicting things? On the one hand, I gratefully want to please God and yet, at the same time, I want those very things He sacrificed so much to forgive? It seems reasonable to think that what we are convinced is true would simply be the way we would live. But the truth is that the mind is a battleground of unparalleled proportions; our conflicting desires rage within us.

Even the Apostle Paul experienced this same struggle with his flesh. We are all continually engaged in spiritual mental battles against the powerfully oppressive influences of the flesh, the world and the devil—and even the effects of our own false presuppositions: **But I see another law in my members, warring against the law of my mind, and bringing me into captivity to the law of sin which is in my members** (Romans 7:23).

In His word, God shows us that our heart and mind are linked together. We often read about "thinking in our heart" in the Bible (Zechariah 8:17; Philippians 1:7; Deuteronomy 9:4; Esther 4:13). As we dwell on an idea, we eventually come to a conclusion about it. However, because of the noetic effect of sin,[10] that conclusion will likely be corrupt in part or in whole. When we reason or rationalize that something is good or true, it follows that we believe it is a good

---

10 www.theopedida.com/Noetic_effects_of_sin: Noetic effects of sin are the ways that sin negatively affects and undermines the human mind and intellect.

thing for our lives. We then develop a conviction that it can or should be a part of our life experience. This place of deepest conviction is our heart and Jesus said that out of our heart come our actions: **But what comes out of the mouth proceeds from the heart, and this defiles a person** (Matthew 15:18).

What our mind dwells on will come to rule our heart (our desires). The Bible never tells us to follow our hearts but instead to keep, direct, guide, and guard our hearts: **Keep your heart with all diligence, for out of it spring the issues of life** (Proverbs 4:23). It is the Christian's responsibility to keep his heart and to direct his thinking upon the Word of God and truth rather than the lies of this world. Thankfully, the Holy Spirit does a supernatural work in our heart and mind which is a major point of the New Covenant according to Hebrews 8:10 and Ezekiel 36:26-27: **For this is the covenant that I will make with the house of Israel after those days, says the Lord: I will put my laws in their mind and write them on their hearts; and I will be their God and they shall be my people.**

The Purpose of Change

In Romans 12:1-2, Paul gives us an outline for counseling someone, to change how they live by changing how they think, so that it conforms to the thoughts of God as written in the Scriptures: **I appeal to you therefore, brothers, by the mercies of God, to present your bodies as a living sacrifice, holy and acceptable to God, which is your spiritual worship. Do not be conformed to this world, but be transformed by the renewal of your mind, that by testing you may discern what is the will of God, what is good and acceptable and perfect.**

In the first two verses of Romans 12, Paul appeals to the Romans, and thereby every Christian, to present our bodies (and so our lives) to God sacrificially, in light of His amazing grace. The "therefore" in Romans 12:1 points to the reason we are to sacrificially present our bodies and to be transformed by renewing our mind. In Romans 11:36, Paul celebrated our salvation and concluded the chapter with a beautiful doxology: **For of Him and through Him and to Him are all things, to whom be glory forever.** He connected our need to sacrifice our desires with the reason that we should do it. Paraphrased, Paul said, "BECAUSE God did so many amazing things to bring about your salvation, and BECAUSE He is exalted above all creation and is more excellent, wise, powerful and just than all others, we must serve this Great King with everything that is in us. Let us lay down our lives, not necessarily in death of body but in death of selfishness, of sin, and live our lives in all ways through all days as Christ would live them, and in this way we will be pleasing our Father."

Ultimately, this means that because we have been purchased by His blood, we are to live our lives in loving, joyful and complete surrender and obedience to His commandments to do His will. We are now responsible to direct our thoughts toward eternity and the promises of God. When counseling, unless a counselee's greatest desire and life guiding goal is to serve, love and please God, we will see very little lasting change in his conduct. When a person truly surrenders control of his life to follow God, he will begin to look more and more like Christ. Since our thoughts are naturally self-serving, we must learn to put on the mind of Christ by directing our hearts for the renewing of our minds concerning every life situation. Proverbs 23:19 reminds us: **Hear, my son, and be wise, and direct your heart in the way.**

We can only present our bodies to God sacrificially if we have the Holy Spirit in us to empower us to die to our selfish desires, also called our "flesh," as Paul explained in Romans 6:11-13: **So you also must consider yourselves dead to sin and alive to God in Christ Jesus. Let not sin therefore reign in your mortal body, to make you obey its passions. Do not present your members to sin as instruments for unrighteousness, but present yourselves to God as those who have been brought from death to life, and your members to God as instruments for righteousness.**

In the command in Romans 12:1-2, Paul also admonishes believers to present their bodies as holy (godly). We must separate from the perspectives, values, and practices of the world. Not only are we to separate ourselves *from* the wisdom of this age, we are to separate ourselves *to* God in a way that is pleasing and acceptable to Him (1 Corinthians 3:18-23). To do this, we must think of God as He truly is and ourselves as we truly are. When we *begin* to think about God and ourselves as He thinks, we will gain a humility before Him that allows us to learn to live the way that Paul described in Romans 12:1-2 and correlates with Isaiah 66:2: **. . . But this is the one to whom I will look: he who is humble and contrite in spirit and trembles at My word.**

Paul reminds us that the sacrifice made by the Father and Son to rescue us from our sins and condemnation was so much greater than any sacrifice we will ever be called to make. Therefore complete surrender of our body and our will to His will is simply reasonable (Romans 12:1).

The Process of Change

In Romans 12:2, the apostle explains how this change is accomplished. When we are renewed in our mind, we will cease to live in conformity to this world, which means that we will not allow the ideals, values, and standards that rule the unconverted world to rule us. The wisdom of the world is derived from priorities and values that are hostile to God because it is a world view rooted in wisdom formed without regard for the Creator. In Second Corinthians 4:4 we are reminded that the god of this age (Satan) has blinded the minds of those who do not believe and thereby has filled the world with indifference for the things of God. Jesus freed us from the spirit that so strongly influences this age. This is the implication of Galatians 1:4: **[Jesus] who gave Himself for our sins to deliver us from the present evil age, according to the will of our God and Father.**

Christ gave Himself for us on the cross to redeem us from the curse of our sins and to deliver us from thinking and living like this evil age, according to its power and perspectives. This amazing act of love and mercy should compel us to give ourselves to God. He gave us the Holy Spirit to teach us God's truth through Scripture, which exposes the propaganda of the Father of Lies (John 8:43-44).

Those who have been set free by the gospel of Christ should be joyfully motivated to turn their back on their former slave master and embrace their new loving and gracious Master with a grateful heart (Galatians 4:8-9). Paul taught us that **. . . the grace of God that brings salvation has appeared to all men, teaching us that, denying ungodliness and worldly lusts, we should live soberly,**

68

righteously, and godly in the present age (Titus 2:11-12). The more we are renewed in our mind to think like Christ, the more we will be renewed in our lifestyle to live like Christ.

Before conversion to Christianity, our lives were conformed to a carnal and godless lifestyle because our minds had a godless worldview. Now, as regenerated believers, there is hope that we no longer have to think carnally but have been given a new worldview with Christ as the central focus. As we learn to direct our hearts by yielding ourselves to the Holy Spirit rather than to the flesh, Romans 8:4-8 provides us with insight about being truly transformed: **. . . in order that the righteous requirement of the law might be fulfilled in us, who walk not according to the flesh but according to the Spirit. For those who live according to the flesh set their minds on the things of the flesh, but those who live according to the Spirit set their minds on the things of the Spirit. To set the mind on the flesh is death, but to set the mind on the Spirit is life and peace. For the mind that is set on the flesh is hostile to God, for it does not submit to God's law; indeed, it cannot. Those who are in the flesh cannot please God.** Those who are in the flesh (carnal) cannot please God. We therefore conclude that only those who are born again by the Spirit are able to be truly transformed by the Word.

Ephesians 4:17-24 provides us with the real hope of transformation into Christ-likeness by the power of the Holy Spirit within us when we cooperate by directing our hearts and minds to adopt new thoughts, the thoughts of God as revealed in Scripture: **All who have believed the gospel unto salvation have had the blinders of their minds removed by the Spirit of God and have been set free to become like Him. This newly opened heart and mind is the beginning of renewing the mind to overcome what the mind has learned while under the influence of the spirit of the age. The renewing of the believer's mind and heart will result in a new walk with God.**

Our deepest motivations from birth are corrupt (Ephesians 2:3) and we are convinced that whatever gratifies is good. This drives actions motivated by a self-serving heart that willingly conforms to the wisdom of the world, since it promotes self-centeredness, *operating as if there is no God.* We gladly embrace the idea that we ourselves are "the gods" we need, as affirmed by the world and the devil. Therefore, if our mind is not being renewed and transformed by the Spirit through the Word, we will continue to conform to the world.

The original tense of the Romans 12:1-2 passage is both interesting and enlightening. Both "conformed" and "transformed" in Romans 12:2 are in *Present Passive Imperative tense*.[11] These concepts both show an action that is being done to the subject. Paul shows us that we will either be continuing to be conformed into the image of the world, or we will be sanctified by being transformed into the image of Christ.

The Word of God, which changes us by transforming us from carnal to Christ-like, affirms that we cannot understand our purpose or our duty unless it is revealed from another source. We are revelation receivers. Paul Tripp, in his excellent book, *Instruments in the Redeemer's Hands,* instructs us that:

> . . . Adam and Eve were created to be Revelation receivers . . . . They were created with the ability to hear, understand, and apply God's word to their lives. These abilities were not given primarily to encourage human relationships. They were given so that we could know God and understand him.[12]

Therefore, we must be diligent to study the Word for our lives to be approved by God.

Our Responsibility

In Luke 10:27 we are told that we are to love the Lord our God with all our heart, soul, strength and mind. The truth is that if we don't love God with all of our minds, we will be unable to love Him with all of our heart and soul and strength.

---

11 Robertson, Archibald Thomas, A.M., D.D., LL.D., Litt. D., *Word Pictures in the New Testament*, (Nashville, Broadman Press, 1930), WORD*search* CROSS e-book, under: "Romans 12:2".

12 Tripp, Paul David, *Instruments in the Redeemer's Hands*, (Phillipsburg, NJ, P & R Publishing, 2002), p. 40.

We are in a war against our flesh on the battlefield of our minds. Once the Spirit of God has made the Word of God effective in our minds we are given the responsibility to continue this process of growing in Christ (Colossians 2:18). Scripture assures us that if we are genuinely regenerated we will be made into the image of Christ (Romans 8:28-30). When we are not motivated to progress in this sanctification, God will intervene in our lives with discipline to motivate us (Hebrews 12:5-13). We are reminded in this text that no discipline **"seems to be joyful for the present, but painful; nevertheless, afterward it yields the peaceable fruit of righteousness to those who have been trained by it."**

God is going to sanctify His children and the process can be more or less pleasant depending on our cooperation. Our cooperation or lack of it shows up in our choices. In Romans 12:1-2, Paul commands us to choose our influences. It is important that as His children we make wise choices. Quality and quantity of influence either conform us passively or transform us by His power. The quality of influence, either godly or worldly, will shape the mind, heart, and life as we choose to allow it to permeate our thinking. The quantity of time we spend being influenced by godly or worldly influence will ultimately and proportionately affect the way we think and live.

It is our responsibility to yield our hearts and minds to please God and not ourselves in each situation. It is not reasonable to think that God is going to do for us what He has commanded us to do. In other words, He is not going to command us to do something and then do it Himself. Would it seem reasonable for a parent to instruct a child to eat his vegetables and then eat the vegetables for him? Neither does it seem reasonable to imagine God telling us as His children to do those things that are good for us and then doing them for us or zapping them done in us. That would not promote our sanctification, or spiritual growth.

Since there is no way to totally escape the influence of worldly thinking, we must choose to direct our hearts and minds to God's Word. In this world, we are bombarded with music, books, movies, commercials, TV programming, teachers, friends and family, to mention just a few of the sources that expose us to man-centered wisdom and influence. However, in the times when we can freely choose the type of influence we subject ourselves to, we do not have to and should not choose the worldly type of entertainment that has ungodly messages. To do so will surely continue to conform us to this world, thereby hindering our sanctification.

Free to choose our influences, we should be disciplined to choose toward godliness (2 Corinthians 10:5). There are many godly influences that counter the offers of this world. There are more good books with godly themes available today than you can read in a lifetime. Many Christian organizations and even churches offer movie alternatives that are well produced and good quality with godly themes. If we search with discernment, there is plenty of good, inspiring, Christ-focused music to listen to these days.

Along the line of choosing to listen to godly music, we should also choose our friends wisely because we are often influenced by them. They should be friends that exhort us to love and good works (1 Corinthians 15:33). It is Paul's intention for us to wisely choose the influences that our mind is exposed so that our thinking becomes transformed by those influences.

The thinking of the world tells us that pharmaceutical technology has the answer for our mental anguish, divorce is the answer to marital problems and personal responsibility has become the government's or someone else's problem. These are reasonable arguments for a self-centered/man-centered worldview, but they desire self-exaltation above the knowledge of God (2 Corinthians 10:5). We, as biblical counselors, must not be conformed to the arguments of this age but be transformed by the renewing of our minds that by testing we may discern what is the will of God, what is good and acceptable and perfect (Romans 12:2).

Paul explicitly tells us that the weapons of our warfare have divine power to destroy strongholds (2 Corinthians 10:4). Our primary weapon is the sword of the Spirit (Ephesians 6:17). To compromise biblical teaching with the spirit of the age in counseling is equivalent to dulling the blade of the sword of the Spirit. It is removing the powder from our bullets in this spiritual war of the heart and mind. The Bible is our information source that accomplishes sanctification in us (John 17:17, Ephesians 5:26).

The Scriptures speak often of our responsibility to direct our minds in relationship to our sanctification: **Set your minds on things that are above, not on things that are on earth** (Colossians 3:2-3). The setting of our minds continues the idea of making right "thought" choices (Ephesians 4:17-24; Colossians 3:8-10). If we set our minds on things above, our default becomes thinking about and like Jesus. If our focus is on Christ, then our focus is eternal. Our goals change to eternal goals. If we set our mind on eternal things, earthly things and circumstances will become much more manageable in our mind. Also when our perspectives change to eternal things, our life will better reflect Christ (Philippians 2:3-7).[13]

The Psalmist taught us that meditation and memorization of Scripture will keep us from sin (Psalms 119:9-11, 27, 48; Psalms 1; Joshua 1:8; Malachi 3:16). There are many today who either associate meditation with Eastern mysticism or have no idea what meditation is about. Here is a simple explanation. If you know how to *worry*, you know how to *meditate*. Simply dwell on things above (biblical meditation) as intensely as you dwell on things on the earth (worry). Meditation on Scripture will transform your thinking and your life.

Meditation is more than reading the Bible. "It is possible to encounter a torrential amount of God's truth, though without absorption you will be little better for the experience. Meditation is absorption."[14] Meditative thinking is a powerful tool in renewing our mind. Paul instructs the Philippians about what is proper to meditate on (Philippians 4:8). Renewing our minds through meditation on true, honorable, just, pure, lovely, commendable, excellent, and praiseworthy things will surely keep our thoughts and hearts protected from the spirit of the age and transform us into those Christlike attributes. In fact, Philippians 4:8 is a great passage to test whether what we are thinking about is godly or worldly. If what we are feeding our minds is not in step with this text, it is likely a conforming influence instead of a transforming one.

---

13 More verses addressing an eternal mindset are found in Ephesians 4:17-24, 1 Peter 1:12-16, 1 Peter 4:1-4, Romans 12:2, Colossians 1:21-22, and Philippians 3:16-20. This is just a sample list, but notice that all these texts are commands or warnings against not keeping the commands.

14 Whitney, Donald S., *Spiritual Disciplines for the Christian Life*, (Carol Stream, NavPress, 1991), p.50.

Paul taught us that biblical prayer is a fantastic form of renewing our minds and protecting them from the conforming influence of this age. In Philippians 4:6-7 Paul gives a prime text to remind us of the powerful influence prayer has on renewing our minds. In this context, prayer seems to be the antidote to depression as well as a guard to our hearts (where we believe what we believe at its deepest level) and our minds (where we worry and reason).

As we pray, we should be asking God to fill us with His Spirit and to renew our minds. We should ask the Lord to give us:

- Godly wisdom as opposed to worldly wisdom (James 1:5)
- Help to think as Jesus thinks (Philippians 2:2-5)
- A pure mind (Titus 1:15)
- A mind renewed through understanding of the Scripture (Philippians 1:9-10, Colossians 1:9-10)

Conclusion

The conclusion for Christians is that the mind and heart is where the Spirit of God works in the life of a believer. It is possible, and should be the desire of every believer, to think as Christ thinks. We must remind our counselees and ourselves that the way we direct our thinking will change the way we live. Put another way, the way we are living is a result of the way we are thinking.

God has mercifully given us the tools of His Word and His Spirit for the renewing of our minds. He expects us to yield our minds through personal discipline to use those tools. As we honor and obey Him, He will in turn transform us by renewing our minds into the image of His beloved Son. What a great God we serve!

PERSONAL CONNECTION QUESTIONS

1. As counselors, if we can help our counselees to change the way they think we can help them change the way they live. Journal today how much time you have spent thinking about eternal things vs. temporal things. Estimate as best you can each hour that passes by to see how intentional (transforming) or passive (conforming) your thinking had been.

2. Use the following questions which have been beneficial to me in helping others (counselees) take note of their thinking so they can put off old man in their thought life and put on new man in their thought life:

    a. What were you thinking when you _____?

    b. What goal did you have in mind when you _____?

    c. Does filling your mind with _____ resemble Philippians 4:8?

    d. What should you have been thinking?

    e. If you had been thinking like Jesus, what would you have done differently? (Or, how would Jesus have responded?)

Notes

Chapter 7
PAUL'S MODEL OF CHANGE

Howard Eyrich and Jeffery Young

Now this I say and testify in the Lord, that you must no longer walk as the Gentiles do, in the futility of their minds. They are darkened in their understanding, alienated from the life of God because of the ignorance that is in them, due to their hardness of heart. They have become callous and have given themselves up to sensuality, greedy to practice every kind of impurity. But that is not the way you learned Christ!—assuming that you have heard about him and were taught in him, as the truth is in Jesus, to put off your old self, which belongs to your former manner of life and is corrupt through deceitful desires, and to be renewed in the spirit of your minds, and to put on the new self, created after the likeness of God in true righteousness and holiness.

Ephesians 4:17-24

Introduction to the Heart

While changing people is God responsibility, He has entrusted this concern to capable biblical counselors. Only God can transform the heart and He allows biblical counselors the privilege of sharing that process. Here are examples of three people in typical life situations.[15]

1. Joe was an 18 year-old young man who lost his temper and ended up being arrested. He came to counseling under the mandate of the court.

---

15 Note that these are not real names but fictitious names assigned to typical cases in biblical counseling to protect the identities of those we have served. Any resemblance to these situations is purely coincidental since we have counseled thousands of people over the years.

2. Susie was a middle aged woman who presented herself as a tired wife: "I've had it. Sixteen years of this misery is enough. I'm getting a divorce even if the church throws me out."

3. Jack and Sarah suffered tragic losses from a natural disaster. When they came for counseling, it appeared as though their marriage was beginning to unravel as a result of the stress.

All these counselees came seeking change. Both couples in #2 and #3 professed faith in Christ. Joe in #1 did not. All these counselees desired to engage in change that would positively impact their lives. The couples assumed they had experienced saving faith in Jesus Christ (born again), and were therefore ready to work on implementing life changes. Careful biblical counselors, however, understand that an assumption of salvation can often be a fallacy that leads to failure. One who is not truly born again will frequently have an inaccurate concept of grace (that invalidates responsibility for change) or tend toward legalism (that becomes self-change by rule keeping).

In all of these cases, Jesus must intervene as He did for the blind man of John 9:25b, who said after his encounter with Jesus: **"One thing I do know, that though I was blind, now I see."** Like him, these counselees are in need of engagement and enlightenment.

Like Christ, Paul knows that believers need Jesus to impact the heart. In Matthew 5:27-28, Jesus addressed the heart directly: **You have heard that it was said, "You shall not commit adultery." But I say to you that everyone who looks at a woman with lustful intent has already committed adultery with her in <u>his heart</u>.** Luke 6:45 (emphasis mine) is another example of Jesus' concern for heart transformation: **The good person <u>out of the good treasure of his heart</u> produces good, and the evil person out of his evil treasure produces evil, for out of the abundance of the heart his mouth speaks** (Matthew 12:35, emphasis mine).

In these two passages, Jesus teaches that the heart of the problem is a problem of the heart. In the same way, before we can help people to change their behavior we must address the issues of their heart. Along the way of life, I [Howard] have had the opportunity to work with three organizations that assisted churches with church conflict. What these organizations learned by interacting with numerous congregations is that church conflict is the result of problems with the hearts of congregants.

Our study of the Scriptures intertwined with our life experience has resulted in the following progressive outline for change from the writings of Paul. Though we will certainly not exhaust the subject, we will observe five steps encapsulated in five words in their progressive nature:

1. Encounter
2. Enlightenment
3. Engagement
4. Exchange
5. Exaltation

We will observe these worked out in the life of the Apostle, forming Paul's model of change.

1. Encounter

Life for Paul begins as the life of Saul. In our modern world, Saul would have been the equivalent of a Harvard PhD in Old Testament serving as the Executive Director of the Jewish League for Religious Purity. He was a highly influential man. He was a radical within his own circles. But then, he is encountered by Jesus on the Damascus Road. He is regenerated and he later becomes Paul the Apostle (Acts 13:9).

Before his encounter with Jesus, Saul was a cultural believer. Listen to what he says in Acts 23:6: **"I am a Pharisee of the Pharisees."** In Acts 22:3, he says: **"I am truly a man which am a Jew born in Tarsus, a city of Cilicia, yet brought up in this city [Jerusalem] at the feet of Gamaliel, and taught according to the perfect manner of the law of the fathers, and was zealous towards God, as you all are this day."** Saul was a keeper of the law. When he says "I am a Pharisee of the Pharisees" he means that nobody had done a better job of performing the expected religious duty. To put it in our contemporary church context, he was in church Sunday and Wednesday. He was in men's Bible study. He had memorized whole books of the Bible. He was on a team to serve the widows in the congregation. He was an elder or deacon. He appeared to be the model Jew because of his religious commitment.

Many people who are in the church today are religious, cultural believers just like Saul. They attend church and Sunday school regularly. They have their children baptized. They encourage, even require, children to attend Vacation Bible Schools, catechism camps, and youth groups. They often attend Bible studies and may even lead Bible studies, but they have not had an encounter with Jesus. When these people seek counsel or assistance from the pastor, he begins by honoring their profession of faith. But, if he is alert he will listen to discern if they have been encountered by Jesus. You see, if they have not had an encounter with Jesus, then they are dead in their sin, like Saul, and incapable of living a Christian life. They do not have the Holy Spirit to empower them to change. They have heart problems!

Jesus had previously confronted another Jewish leader named Nicodemus, who came to Jesus by night and likely represented a contingency from the Sanhedrin. Remember the encounter with Nicodemus when Jesus said in John 3:5: **"Truly, truly, I say to you, unless one is born of water and the Spirit, he cannot enter into the kingdom of God."**

The concept of change, or as Paul puts it in another passage, *transformation* (Romans 12:1-2), is the process of becoming more and more like Jesus. That is, becoming holy, or set apart. Peter quotes Leviticus 11:44 in 1 Peter 1:16 when he says: **. . . since it is written, "you shall be holy; for I am holy."** God is holy because all of his attributes function in perfect harmony with his character at all times. Therefore, for us to be holy means that all of our being functions in perfect harmony with the character of God. Holiness is to be our goal, which comes to fruition when we see Jesus (1 John 3:2).

The first and essential step in moving toward holiness is to experience an encounter with Jesus whereby we are, as Jesus described it to Nicodemus, born of the Spirit. We are all born dead in our sins and completely lacking in holiness. The new birth is the first step. Unfortunately, all too often, today's professing Christians are modern Pharisees. They have a lot of religious knowledge, but they have not been encountered by Jesus. The new birth is the first step to genuine change. It is a heart transplant (Ezekiel 36:26; 2 Corinthians. 5:17).

2. Enlightenment

Some time ago, we saw an interview with former Vice President Dick Cheney. Several months earlier he had experienced a heart transplant. Somewhere in that interview he said, "I am a new man." However, I noted two striking observations. First, his physical characteristics had not changed. Second, it was necessary for him to maintain that new heart by proper living. When asked if he would attend the Republican Convention, he indicated that he would forego the stress and play golf instead. In the same manner when we are born again, our physical characteristics do not change. Also, our new heart must be cared for and properly supported. Enlightenment in the new life of a Christian can be gained only through our abiding in Christ (John 15:1-5) as we read, study, and obey His Word of truth. Enlightenment has three dimensions:

<u>First Dimension</u>

The first dimension of enlightenment is Lordship. It leads us to the conclusion that the one who encounters us is the <u>Lord</u>. Before becoming Paul, Saul cries out in Acts 9:5: **"Who are you, Lord!"** Like Saul, not all Christians immediately perceive that He is Lord, but we must all come to the realization that there is no such thing as "easy believe-ism" in which we encounter him as Savior but not Lord. Before we can move forward in transformation we must acknowledge him as Lord and recognize that <u>He has the right to direct our lives</u>. Jesus told Saul what to do immediately in Acts 9:5-6: **And he said, "Who are you, Lord?" And he said, "I am Jesus, whom you are persecuting. But rise and enter the city, and you will be told what you are to do."** Recognizing Jesus as the Lord means that we set aside our desires to be obedient to his desires.

As biblical counselors, we have observed that marriage mates must learn to set aside their many self-desires in order to fulfill Jesus' command for them to be a godly mate. Idolatrous desires for such things as guns, cars, clothing, or house décor as well as our God-given gifts and talents must come under the Lordship of Christ. The Apostle Paul noted that all his assets became as rubbish compared to the surpassing value of knowing Jesus Christ as Lord (Philippians 3:8-9).

Second Dimension

The second dimension of enlightenment is commissioning. Immediately Paul responded to God's direction above and went into the city. There he meets with Ananias and is soon commissioned to service. No matter how bad we are or we think we are, as illustrated by the demoniac in Mark 8, when we are encountered by Jesus, He says to us as He did to him in Mark 8:19: **"Go home to your people and report to them what great things the Lord has done for you and he had mercy on you."** In the Apostle Paul's thinking, there are two facets of commissioning. The first is the commission as disciple-maker (Matthew 28:18-20). The second is character transformation. Paul puts it this way in 1 Thessalonians 4:3: **"This is the will of God, your sanctification."** He then defines this sanctification, or spiritual growth, as a changed life (1Thessalonians 4:4-8).

Third Dimension

The third dimension of enlightenment is commitment. We find in Acts 9:20 that Paul was immediately called to obedience. We see this in that he began to preach about Jesus immediately. He laid down his Jewish flag and picked up the Christian flag, so to speak.[16] This was so evident in Susie's husband (#2). He was a self-made man who was unaccustomed to adjusting his lifestyle for the sake of others. Within a couple of months of his conversion, his commitment became evident in his willingness to be obedient to the Word in relationship to his wife.

3. Engagement

Encounter and enlightenment must be followed by engagement with the Word of God and theology. Encounter without engagement produces a Christian who lives in the same old way. Paul refers to this as the *old man*. For me (Howard), a youth ignorant of the Bible, it took four years at a Christian University, youth group at church, and various ministry opportunities that called for study of the Word

---

16 I (Howard) became a believer on Labor Day weekend of my 17th year. Within a week I stopped smoking. By mid-fall my mentor had me serving on a committee of our youth group. On New Year's Eve I preached my first sermon. I had been encountered by Jesus and my mentor led me into enlightenment and moved me into engagement with the Word of God.

gaining theological understanding, before I became informed about the nature of my sinful heart and the power of the Gospel. Without knowledge of the Word and a theological understanding of the faith, we will not have the tools for change and it is not likely that we will change. That is, we will not come to understand the full implications of the Gospel. We may have a lot of religious emotion, but we will have little of the transformation of which Paul speaks in Romans 12:1-2. This lack of transformation is a great deficit that we meet in many counselees.

Engagement with the Word and a theological appreciation for the consistency of the Christian faith is necessary to know how God would have us change. Studying Scripture is necessary to understand the process of biblical change.

For the Apostle Paul there was a two to three year period in the Arabian Desert where the Lord met with him in some fashion and reconfigured his Pharisaical views of the Old Testament by the teachings of Jesus. It is during this time that Paul worked out the great truths that he penned in Romans and the Prison Epistles.

For me (Jeff), my earliest enlightenment from the Word of God came as I was seeking desperately to find peace, strength, and comfort when facing trials of any kind. The 23rd Psalm is my first memory of an encouraging portion of Scripture. As a youth, I would read this passage before a big ball game or in the midst of a big trial of some kind. After I was encountered by Jesus at age 20, the first Scripture passage that I can remember memorizing and being deeply impacted by was John 14:27: **Peace I leave with you; my peace I give to you. Not as the world gives do I give you. Let not your hearts be troubled, neither let them be afraid.** The things of this world, or of the flesh, no matter how satisfying they seemed to be at the moment, were only temporary and never brought me peace of mind or lasting pleasure.

Engagement with the Word of God confirmed that only Jesus Christ, the Prince of Peace, can bring lasting peace. After my conversion, I (Jeff) plunged into God's Word, reading it voraciously and digesting its teaching (experiencing what Paul writes in 2 Timothy 3:16-17). In the process, the life-impacting and life-changing power of God's Word brought a renewing of my mind, effecting a transformation that Paul calls putting on of the new man (Ephesians 4:24, KJV).

4. Exchanged Life (Ephesians 4:17-24)

Now we are ready to discuss the *mechanics* of change. When we have been encountered by Jesus, experienced enlightenment, and engaged with the Word of God, we can begin to live an **exchanged life. That is, since we have put off the old man's sinful nature and replaced it with the** power of the Holy Spirit, we can now begin putting off the behavior of the old man and exchanging that life for the new life in Christ.

The Facts of the Exchanged Life

The Bible says that we put on the *new man.* Note Ephesians 4:20-21: **But that is not the way you learned Christ! —assuming that you have heard about him and were taught in him, as the truth is in Jesus.** The way a person lived life before Christ is not the way a person lives life after Christ (Luke 6:45-49). Allow me to paraphrase Paul, here in Ephesians 4:20-21: "I am assuming that you have been encountered by Christ (that is, you have a new heart), that you have been enlightened (that is you have acknowledged his Lordship, understood your commission and made your commitment to serve him), and that you have engaged the Word of God and gained a theological understanding." Therefore, the facts of implementing the exchanged life are these in the next verse in the passage, Ephesians 4:22-24 . . . **to put off your old self, which belongs to your former manner of life and is corrupt through deceitful desires, and to be renewed in the spirit of your minds, and to put on the new self, created after the likeness of God in true righteousness and holiness.**

The Power for the Exchanged Life

Luke 4:14 and Hebrews 2:14-18 shed light on the power of the exchanged life. Luke 4:14 simply states: **And Jesus returned in the power of the Spirit to Galilee, and a report about him went out through all the surrounding country.** From this verse and the Hebrews 2 passage, it is impossible not to conclude that Jesus was dependent upon the Holy Spirit.

If Jesus was dependent upon the Holy Spirit, then surely we must be also. As the Holy Spirit symbolically descended upon Jesus at His baptism, so the Holy Spirit descends upon our souls at the new birth. Paul picks up this theme in Romans 8 after raising the question in Romans 7:24: **"Wretched man that I am! Who will set me free from the body of this death?"** He continues by answering this question in Romans 7:25-8:1-2: **"Thanks be to God through Jesus Christ our Lord! So then, I myself serve the law of God with my mind, but with my flesh I serve the law of sin. There is therefore now no condemnation for those who are in Christ Jesus. For the law of the (Holy) Spirit of life in Christ Jesus has set you free from the law of sin and death (the old man)."**

In other words, Paul is saying now put on the new man since **"the Spirit of Him who raised Jesus from the dead dwells in you, He who raised Christ Jesus from the dead will also give life to your mortal bodies through His Spirit who indwells you"** (Romans 8:11). **"Hence, brethren, we are under no obligation to the flesh (old man), to love according to the flesh** (lusts of deceit, Ephesians 4:22) **if by the Spirit you are putting to death the deeds of the body you will live** (put on the new man). **For all who are being led by the Spirit of God, these are sons of God"** (Romans 8:13-14).

In other words, Paul is indicating that as we were saved by grace so we are undergoing sanctification by grace. That is, what Paul describes in Romans 8:29 as **to be conformed to the image of his son** and Romans 12:2 as **transformed by the renewing of your mind** and 2 Corinthians 3:18 **we . . . are being transformed into the image from one degree of glory to another**[17] is to take place as spiritual growth.

In salvation we were regenerated by God (wholly the work of God) and thereby enabled to express faith in Christ as our redeemer. So in sanctification, we are baptized by the Holy Spirit and thereby *enabled to be obedient* (that is, we put off the old man, undergo continual renewing of our minds, and we put on the new man—

---

17 Strong's Concordance defines grace as the Divine influence upon the heart, and its reflection in the life. Vines Expository Dictionary of Greek words defines grace as the Divine favor that practically affects the spiritual state of those who have experienced its exercise; empowering and equipping them for service.

living obediently).[18] The Westminster Confession of Faith sums up sanctification in these words: "Sanctification is the work of God's grace, whereby we are renewed in the whole man after the image of God, and we are enabled more and more to die unto sin, and live unto righteousness" (WCF 9.35).

The Results of the Exchanged Life in the Four Spheres of Life

Paul outlines the desired results of this exchanged life in the four spheres of life. In 1Thessalonians 4:3-8, Paul outlines how this process is to be manifested in our *personal lives*. He tells us explicitly that the will of God for our lives is our sanctification. He uses sexuality, the dimension of life with which human beings universally struggle, as his illustration. Abstain ("put off") and control ("put on") the new man. Verses five through seven embody the renewed thinking and verse nine makes it clear that the Holy Spirit is actively empowering us; and therefore, to not move towards sanctification is to disregard God's graceful enablement by the Holy Spirit.

Whether two sweet female servants in Philippi or the litigious individuals in Corinth, it is obvious even in the churches under Paul's leadership that there was a desperate need for sanctified behavioral change in *church relationships*. Paul addresses numerous areas of concern, but especially these three:

1. Improper treatment of pastors is addressed in his direction to give double honor to those who labor in the Word (1 Timothy 5:17)

2. Inappropriate lack of respect for those who rule over the church (Hebrews 13:17)

3. Importance of generational relationships and transference of values (Titus 2:1-8)

---

18 The contemporary debates over the grace issue seems to be a result of attempts to get further inside the "head of God" to explain the complexity of the relationship between human responsibility and Divine work than God has been pleased to reveal. As a result the representatives of both sides often fail to display grace. We are suggesting that Paul affirms grace mediated by the Holy Spirit as essential to the exercise of human responsibility in sanctification and that we are to join him in engaging in responsible living by the power of the Spirit.

The fourth sphere of life regards the way we behave in the *public square* (Jeremiah 29:7; Titus 3). Paul and Peter both recognize that as believers we are aliens in this world. We have been commissioned as ambassadors by the King. So, like Israel living in an alien city, we are to pray for and engage with the citizenry. We should look like Daniel and his three friends (Daniel 3 and 4). In the Titus 3 passage Paul reminds us that we are saved by grace (v. 5) and that because the Holy Spirit has been poured out on us we should be **"careful to devote (ourselves) to good works"** (v. 8). Even in the way we live in the public square, there is the divine mystery of the inner face of God's working and our responsibility for obedience empowered by God. Here we have Paul's model of change articulated once again.

5. Exaltation of Christ

An exchanged way of life is marked by the motivation to exalt Christ in all things. A great test of the consistency of our Christian life can be measured by the little everyday personal management matters articulated by these questions:

- How do I think about people who are less fortunate than I am?
- How do I think about people who struggle with weight problems?
- How do I think about the person with a disability?
- How do I react when the person working the checkout counter seems incompetent and is holding up the line and I'm in a hurry?
- How do I treat people with whom I differ?

You see, the Christian life is about transformation that begins with a heart transplant when we are encountered by Jesus. The Christian life is about change. The Christian life is about holiness. Transformation, change, and holiness are all synonyms. The way I think or react to all people and to every situation in life should be defined by this question: Will my thoughts and actions exalt Christ and glorify God?

Once known as President Nixon's "hatchet man," Charles Colson gained notoriety at the height of the Watergate, being named as one of the Watergate Seven. Colson's mid-life encounter with Christ sparked a radical life change. His early links with R. C. Sproul and Sproul's book, *The Holiness of God*, served as his engagement. Through good engagement Colson learned the great truths of which we speak today and, as a result, you can see the tracks of a heart change just like you can see the tracks of a heart change in the Apostle Paul. Colson's enlightenment had already begun in prison where he observed the need for a radically different approach in the justice system. He came to realize that the needed radical change began with a gospel encounter. In the public square his life evidenced the exchange of the new man for the old man. As a result his transformed life became a great example of a life motivated by the desire to glorify God.

Conclusion

So, what about our typical Christian counselees from the beginning of this chapter?

1. Joe: The counselor utilized a two pronged approach with Joe. First, a workbook on anger management was used to satisfy the court and provide a discussion generator. In discussing the workbook, the counselor took his lead from Isaiah 1:8: **"Come now, let us reason together," says the Lord: "though your sins are like scarlet, they shall be as white as snow . . . ."** Second, from the workbook, a process of evangelism was developed with the intention to lead him towards an encounter with Jesus.

2. Susie: She was persuaded to postpone her intended divorce proceedings. Her husband was contacted by two elders and he agreed to counseling. Through evangelism in the counseling process, he was encountered by Christ. He engaged with the Word of God and as a result he began to take seriously his responsibilities as a husband. While there were certainly tensions along the way, church discipline was avoided and growth developed so that today they are a happily married couple integrated into their church.

3. Jack and Sarah: They suffered tragic loss. It appeared that the marriage started to unravel as a result of the stress. At least, this is

what they presented when coming to counseling. But in reality, there were a whole string of "old man" behaviors on both their parts that dominated their relationship. Engagement with the Word of God brought enlightenment resulting in repentance and awareness that the indwelling Holy Spirit would empower them for obedience. As a result, they both began to put off these old man behaviors and put on new man behaviors as their minds were renewed through engagement with the Word of God. They began to take ownership for their sin and express repentance. As they experienced the gracious work of the Holy Spirit in the transformation of their minds, their motivation became the glory of God rather than their self-satisfaction. They were more and more enabled to put on the new man and, as a result, their marriage was revived and renewed.

These typical cases illustrate Paul's model for change that begins with a heart transplant (encounter with Jesus), is facilitated by enlightenment and engagement empowered by the Holy Spirit, and observed in lives motivated to express the glory of God in every dimension of life (exchanged lives for exaltation of Christ).

PERSONAL CONNECTION QUESTIONS

1. How do you know if you have truly been "born again"? Are you different now than before the moment you encountered Christ? If so, how? List the ways now, to be reminded of the transformational power of the Gospel.

2. How are you going to engage more with the Word of God? Develop a simple Bible study plan to implement immediately if you do not have one already. A failure to plan often becomes a planned failure.

Notes

Chapter 8
BLESSING THE COUNSELEE

Bob Froese

To all who are in Rome, beloved of God, called to be saints: Grace to you and peace from God our Father and the Lord Jesus Christ
Romans 1:7

To the saints and faithful brethren in Christ who are in Colossae: Grace to you and peace from God our Father and the Lord Jesus Christ
Colossians 1:2

Every 4th of July, the United States of America celebrates Independence Day. Across the country, people gather for parades, picnics, and fireworks to celebrate one day in 1776 when America became a sovereign nation, united in freedom from British rule. Yet while the United States of America celebrates independence as a nation, Americans are rapidly running in different directions in pursuit of peace they mistakenly believe is found in personal fulfillment, pursuing whatever lifestyle they believe will satisfy that yearning.

As well as personal fulfillment and satisfaction, people reveal themselves to be obsessed with the pursuit of independence that they mistakenly believe will bring true peace. News reports and television talk shows center upon nations seeking their independence and peace amid the turbulent times in which they live. People are moving in different directions, but all appear to be seeking the same goal—a life of fulfillment, a life of satisfaction, a life of total independence where each one can do as he or she pleases. Indeed it appears that the aim of society down through history has been to somehow manufacture a culture in which each member can enjoy the safety and comfort that a sovereign nation can supply.

The climate of Paul's time was no different. And Paul, who had been radically saved and subsequently given a pastor's shepherding heart by the Holy Spirit, deeply desired to bless those he held close in his heart. How would he actually bless those he loved?

Would he provide secrets for personal satisfaction, fulfillment, and independence leading to peace? The answer to finding true peace is only found in a life completely surrendered and dependent on Jesus Christ, in complete reliance upon Him and His body, the church, or people of God.

Paul's Greetings

Paul's letters to the believers in two very cutting-edge cities of their day, Rome and Colossae, start with the following greetings: **To all who are in Rome, beloved of God, called to be saints: Grace to you and peace from God our Father and the Lord Jesus Christ** (Romans 1:7), and **To the saints and faithful brethren in Christ who are in Colossae: Grace to you and peace from God our Father and the Lord Jesus Christ** (Colossians 1:2). This greeting of grace, referring to the unmerited favor of God, was the common greeting used by Greeks. The greeting of peace, referring to peace from God our Father and our Lord Jesus Christ, was the common greeting Jews would use. These dual greetings indicate the mixed ethnicity of the churches at Rome and Colossae. Independently, the greetings may not have been complete theologically, but together they represent the fullness of the Gospel message. It's impossible to experience the peace from God without first experiencing the grace of God in salvation!

The faith of these mixed ethnic groups of Christians was becoming well known to the surrounding lands and countrymen. Paul realized that it would not be long before they experienced an invasion of false teachers who desired to infiltrate the church. It is on this premise that Paul writes to the faithful disciples of Jesus Christ in Rome and Colossae, bound together with them *dependently* in the unity of the body of Christ. They would need one another vitally in days ahead as persecution would rise and peace would seem unattainable.

What Paul understood was that the peace people sought—which is no different from the peace people seek today—is not an independent peace but rather a *dependent* peace. This peace is generated from a life devoted to and dependent on a relationship with the God of the Bible, through the atoning death, burial and resurrection of Jesus Christ. At the very onset of his letters in his greetings to these two churches, he masterfully articulates three vital elements of biblical counseling: dependence on God, grace, and peace.

First of all, citizens of the kingdom of Christ, whom Paul describes as **"saints," "beloved of God," "saints, faithful brethren,"** become one not by independence, but dependence on God. Secondly, with God as the source of righteousness, as love is received through Jesus Christ, **"grace to you"** is poured out as unmerited favor. Finally, Paul speaks of the result of walking in the grace of God through Christ as **"peace from God."** These three foundations of biblical counseling are alive and well nearly two thousand years later.

Paul declares to these Christians the fact of their spiritual privilege solidified in eternity past. He focuses attention on how they became saints, referring to their spiritual privilege in the present. When he speaks of them as those called to be saints, by way of the sovereign call of God upon their individual lives, he is reminding them of the fact that God had chosen them personally to enter into a glorious relationship with Him through the redemptive work of His only begotten Son, Jesus Christ (Romans 8:29).

Through personal disciple-making, the spiritually-maturing Christian learns to find peace even in adversity and in the midst of suffering. Think of the counselee who shows up with the desire to be released from his trial or affliction, hoping to be set on the pathway to what he truly seeks—a little peace and joy. He believes that if somehow he could be released from this struggle his life will be easier and thus more livable. Although the new Christian is looking for something more practical in nature, Paul takes a radically different stance in identifying the three basic needs of every man: dependence on God, grace, and peace. Unlike wealth, pleasure, fame or even health, these three necessary elements are progressive in nature; each flows from the previous one.

1. Dependence on God Alone

The first basic need of man, which ultimately leads to finding true peace, is to learn to trust, or depend upon, God alone. Christians must be discipled to learn how to trust in God on a daily, practical basis. Dependence upon God alone begins with a singular focus on God as the source of righteousness. That focus cannot be divided between the eternal and the temporal. In both greetings in Romans 1:7 and Colossians 1:2, Paul addresses the Christians as "saints" because he is reminding them of their singular focus upon the eternal and never-fading promises of God.

Saints are citizens of Heaven, and there is no unrighteousness in God's perfect Heaven (Romans 1:18, 1 Corinthians 6:9). Saints receive the love of God through the grace provided in the forgiveness of Jesus Christ. In the Greek language, grace is *charis*, which means the unmerited favor of God. No individual can have peace apart from knowing the *charis* of God, a knowledge that begins with realizing and acknowledging God as the very source of righteousness. The life of peace through the grace of God in Christ is founded on total dependence upon God as the source of righteousness.

Paul points his counselees to the foundational truth that God is the source of love (Romans 8:35-39; 1 John 4:7). This is the distinctive mark of a Christian: we have been taken off the throne of our life and God has been elevated to His proper position as Lord. The Bible identifies human beings as walking in one of two dimensions, either the natural state or the spiritual state. Every Christian, though living in the spiritual state in Christ, must also live amid the natural, being in the world but not of it (John 17:15-16). The Christians that physically live in Rome and Colossae spiritually abide in Christ. Within the physical realm, our duties and relationships must be taken seriously with dutiful fulfillment of obligations. But more importantly, a Christian lives **"in Christ"** as a citizen of the kingdom of Christ, as a citizen of Heaven (Ephesians 2:6; Philippians 1:27; 3:20-21).

Paul leads by encouraging these individuals in Rome and Colossae with the fact that they are saints—with citizenship in

Heaven! He longs for them to understand that the blessing God bestows upon His followers is not circumstantial! Though a believer may move physically from place to place in this world, he is in Christ. Though a believer may experience difficult circumstances, he is in Christ. Everything that flows into the life of a believer is based on being in Christ. Happiness, peace and joy are dependent only on being rightly related to Jesus Christ (Romans 8:1). Circumstances in one's life can and will change, but the fact that one is in Christ can never change. Our life may be immersed in persecution, may be much more painful, unpleasant and less prestigious than ever imagined, but the fact that we are in Christ can never change. Rewards may be much less attractive than hoped for, praise may be non-existent from the world, but the fact that we are in Christ can never change. The disciple of Christ diligently and cheerfully serves, without complaining, for one reason—he is dependent on Christ and does all things as unto the Lord.

Each and every believer is living in his own Colossae, his own Rome, in one way or another. Yet each believer's citizenship is secure in Heaven through faith in the finished work of Jesus Christ (Philippians 3:20). Therefore, it is not our circumstances that set the tone for our lives but rather our union with Christ. Paul begins communication with the Christians in Colossae and Rome by naming the identity of each true believer as part of a team with which true believers are identified. Within that team, there is an underlying unity that allows its members to pull on the rope in the same direction. The body of Christ is unified in Christ. Thus, we must adjust our sights from the here and now of earth. We must move our gaze upward towards Heaven, realizing that God is Sovereign, and that everything that occurs in this life has been ordained by God (Colossians 3:1-3; Acts 17:26). Imagine putting on a hockey goalie's mask with the bars in front of your face. When you focus on the bars you cannot see clearly, but when your look past the bars, you can focus on what is in front of you.

It is this union in Christ, this citizenship in Heaven that provides accountability within the body of Christ, His church. Paul refuses to build on any other foundation. Clear commitment to Christ comes first, similar to a team in which everyone wears the same jersey, with the crest of Christ emblazoned across our chests, rather than the personal name and number on the back of the jersey.

Oh, yes, the team of Jesus Christ is embroiled in a battle; it is a war that rages within each and every human being's desire for autonomy and independence. Yet the very essence of Christianity, and the believers' subsequent joy, is total dependence on Jesus Christ. As humans, it is such a temptation to set our gaze on the horizontal. Our eyesight naturally sees the here and now, and what is going on around us. Paul sets the example for biblical counselors to channel the focus of counselees onto the vertical rather than the horizontal. This is accomplished only as we, like Paul, get ourselves out of the way and usher people toward the hope of citizenship in the kingdom of Christ. It is only when this commitment is declared and established that anyone can receive the love of God as the source of love and become a living conduit of His love to others. In Christ, others become the object of God's divinely inspired love.

Paul was well aware that one of the greatest dangers facing professing believers is when mankind is elevated to a position God never intended them to hold. The biggest problem of those in Rome, Colossae, or any city or town today, is a problem with the heart. This dilemma began thousands of years ago with the entry of sin. Who does one trust? Who has been elevated as the source of hope? Only in Christ can human beings hold God in His rightful position, high and lifted up. Today's culture teaches us to place trust in self. This produces a focus on human beings rather than on God, leading one away from grace and peace. An example of this can be seen in the life of Moses.

In the final chapter of Deuteronomy, Moses and Joshua stood and looked over the Promised Land. Although Moses was one of the greatest leaders this world has ever known, he was denied entrance (Deuteronomy 34:1-4). Moses was allowed to set his eyes upon it but not allowed to enter the Promised Land. Imagine, after leading this whining, complaining, rebellious group of people for 40 years, God held Moses back from entering into the land that had been promised, the very goal of the journey. Why did God do this? The answer to this question is found in Numbers 20:1-13, where we read of Moses' sin of self-exaltation at Kadesh. In response to the constant complaining of the people of Israel, Moses uttered the words that cost him his entrance into the Promised Land: **Then Moses and Aaron gathered the assembly together before the rock, and he said to them, "Hear now, you rebels! Shall we bring water for you out of this rock?"** That little two lettered word **"we"** was enough for God to deny Moses entry into the Promised Land. God responded to Moses: **"Because you did not believe in me, to uphold me as holy in the eyes of the people of Israel, therefore you shall not bring this assembly into the land that I have given them."**

The Lord will share His glory with no man (Isaiah 42:8; 48:11)! Why is this so serious? Our view of the seriousness of this sin reveals whether we are thinking biblically regarding who God is and who we are. Self-exaltation is a serious sin. When we become a citizen of Heaven, a saint, one beloved of God, we take humans down from their pedestal and put God in the position He, and He alone, rightfully holds (Isaiah 28:1-2; Proverbs 17:19). Paul reveals his answer to the question regarding the seriousness of this sin, by asking an obvious question. **"But who are you, O man, to answer back to God? Will the molded say to its molder, 'Why have you made me like this?' Has the potter no right over the clay?"** (Romans 9:20-21). Self-exaltation reveals an unbiblical (sinful) view of God and man.

Often counselees are in upheaval because they had trusted someone who let them down. However, not once does God ever teach us to put our trust in other people. Such trust elevates man and lowers God. In Jeremiah 17:5-10, God speaks through His prophet to warn of that very thing. In Proverbs 3:5-6, God describes the pathway to a smooth life, a life that lacks the ups and downs that man-exaltation, or self-exaltation, would bring.

We are all born with a horizontal view. When people are the source of our joy and hope, we all find ourselves in times of chaos and difficulty. What's going on when a life is so drastically affected by others? Man has been elevated above God. When humans occupy the position reserved only for God, they ride the proverbial emotional roller-coaster rather than live out the grace of God and walk in the serenity of peace from God (John 14:27). But God can be the source of love and righteousness, and it is in this confidence that Paul writes, **"saints and faithful brethren in Christ."**

2. The Grace of Jesus Christ

The second basic need of spiritually maturing Christians is learning about the grace of Jesus Christ. In all of his greetings in Romans 1:7, Colossians 1:2, Galatians 1:3, and Ephesians 2:8-10, Paul moves from encouraging the saints by reminding them of *who they are* in Christ to reminding them of *what they have* in Christ. It is the grace of God that each believer depends on to walk in a world that is fallen. It is this grace that the Lord bestows upon a believer when He promises that He will never leave or abandon them.

That does not mean that a believer's life will be easy by any means. But it does mean that God will never give us any more than we can handle *by His grace*. It means that with a trial, the Lord will provide the strength in His Spirit to stand up under it (1 Corinthians 10:13). Paul teaches us that Christians must view trials with the eyes of God's perspective. For those standing in God's grace, trials produce perseverance, character, and ultimately hope (Romans 3:3-5).

While under arrest for preaching the gospel, Paul wrote to the church at Philippi. He used his life as a living picture to explain that trials provide opportunity to magnify Jesus Christ (Philippians 1:20). As the world watched him, they saw little of Jesus' impact on his life until he faced difficulty. But by his response to trials, people caught a glimpse of the glory of Jesus Christ. It is like a football player who catches the winning touchdown pass in the end zone and raises one finger in the air to signify thanks to God. But the testimony that really draws attention to Christ is when a player drops the ball to lose the game and still points that finger to God in true worship. If a believer only thanks God or depends on Him for His grace when things go according to his personal desires, he has a worship problem and is not depending on the grace that God provides.

It is no wonder that Jesus begins His first public sermon with **"Blessed are the poor in spirit, for theirs is the kingdom of Heaven"** (Matthew 5:3). When we consider and admit who we are apart from Christ, upon conviction of the Holy Spirit, we plead guilty. That confession of sin brings us into reconciliation with Christ. This great gift of the grace of God is what a believer depends on daily. Paul exemplifies confession, repentance, and forgiveness as the nourishment that brings comfort for the tried and afflicted soul, all by the grace of God. At times, Christians need to be discipled by a trusted Christian friend to recognize the grace of God in his life and to give thanks for it. Sometimes Christians forget or miss the grace of God and a disciple-making relationship will often provide opportunities to remind a spiritually-growing Christian.

3. Peace from God

> **". . . and <u>peace</u> from God our Father & the Lord Jesus Christ"** (Romans 1:7, emphasis mine). See also Colossians 1:2; Galatians 5:22-23 and Ephesians 2:14-15.

The third basic need of mankind is the peace that only comes from God, since it provides comfort and confidence to a child of God who is walking in regular discipline of Scripture. The only way to experience God's peace is this: out with the old (confession) and in with the new (forgiveness). In daily forgiveness of sin through confession, we worship the Lord for His love for us, Christ's sacrifice for us, and the Holy Spirit's conviction power within us (2 Corinthians 5:14). The result is peace from God.

We can't force people to walk in responsiveness to the Holy Spirit's conviction. When personal desires control us, there can be no peace from God. The mind set on self's goals is death, but the mind set on the Holy Spirit is full of life and peace (Romans 8:6). Biblical counselors help counselees stand down from grasping and clawing at personal desires, confess their desire for control as sin, and surrender to trusting God.

Often counselees are distraught and worried. Difficult situations provide many opportunities to forge ahead in self's desires apart from God's grace. The result is inner chaos and catastrophe. Biblical counselors imitate Paul the Counselor by teaching counselees to:

- Recognize that peace begins with a right relationship with God (Romans 5:1). The peace from God comes by being at peace with God.

- Stop trying to control the situation by placing your demands and expectations on what must change around you that you think will bring you peace. Surrender to the Holy Spirit's conviction of sinful control by confessing it as sin (Romans 8:6).

- Receive God's peace by praying about every decision, evidencing dependent trust in God (Philippians 4:6-7).

- Surrender to the rule of God's peace. This requires thankfulness in all circumstances (Colossians 3:15), even those that are not to your liking. Accept that God has a good plan for His own glory through your trying circumstances and set your mind to be at peace.

- Worship God rather than people (Galatians 1:10). You worship God by trusting Him. You worship self and others when you grasp and claw at control. You are not worshiping God unless peace rules you. Peace is a fruit produced only by the Holy Spirit—so no one can produce peace on their own accord.

If a man possesses the grace of God, the peace of God manifests itself by inner strength and confidence in Christ alone. The peace from God is prerequisite to overcoming the world and walking joyfully in the world, regardless of the circumstances.

Three young Jewish men in Babylon exhibited this inner strength and confidence. King Nebuchadnezzar threatened Shadrach, Meshach, and Abednego with certain death by being thrown into the fiery furnace if they did not bow down to him as lord of their lives. Their reply is evidence of peace from God, composed amid inner strength and confidence. **"Our God whom we serve is able to deliver us from the burning fiery furnace, and He will deliver us out of your hand, O king. But if not, let it be known to you, O king, that we do not serve your gods or worship the golden image that you have set up"** (Daniel 3:17-18).

Conclusion

The greetings in Romans 1:7 and Colossians 1:2 show Paul's desire that believers know their position in Christ and receive the blessings that flow from that wonderful position. The apostle knew his own identity in Christ and his position in Christ motivated him. In 1 Corinthians 5:14-15 he writes, **For the love of Christ controls us, because we have concluded this: that one has died for all, therefore all have died; and he died for all, that those who live might no longer live for themselves but for him who for their sake died and was raised.** He personally knew the riches of God's grace and the comfort of Christ's peace. He longed for those under his care to experience the same.

When counseling fellow believers, biblical counselors should have these same priorities. The end goal of biblical counseling is to build up counselees so that they know who they are in Christ and are equipped for every good work. Toward that end, grace and peace are indispensable. God provides these blessings to His beloved saints not as fringe benefits but as necessary tools to live as aliens and strangers in a hostile environment. Wise counselors will encourage and build up counselees by helping them to understand that they are saints upon whom God has poured His grace and peace.

PERSONAL CONNECTION QUESTIONS

1. Who are you worshiping: self, other people, or God? Who is on the throne in your heart? Are you joyful? Remind yourself of who you are in Christ (**"saints in Christ"**) and what that means for you (**"grace to you and peace from God"**). Can you identify three people who would be encouraged by a reminder of who they are in Christ and what that means for them?

2. Action Assignment: Connect with these three discouraged people. Find out whether they would be willing to have you ask them these five questions below, as you show them the answers in God's Word together. Work through the following questions with them:

Have you been worshiping God or man?
Worship: Revelation 4

Have you been walking in anxiety?
Pray: Philippians 4:6-7

Have you been walking in bitterness?
Forgive: Colossians 3:13

Have you been walking in discouragement?
Walk in Confidence: Psalm 42:5 and 8

Do you need to confess, right now, elevating humans over God?
Confess: 1 John 1:9

Chapter 9
PRESSING ON: LEAVING THE PAST BEHIND

Bill Hines and Mark R. Hines

> **Not that I have already obtained this or am already perfect, but I press on to make it my own, because Christ Jesus has made me his own.**
> Philippians 3:12

Emotionally and spiritually healthy people are able to leave the past behind and press on to a new future, free of encumbrances such as guilt, regret, heartache, and sadness. Whatever we are leaving in the past, the question is: "Can we ever really leave the past behind and live the kind of life God wants for us?" Paul certainly asserts that we can in Philippians 3:12.

In this important verse, notice two things. First, Paul is saying that he lacks perfection. Then he says that his lack of perfection does not hold him back. These points are important to understanding the idea of pressing on. In our ministry of helping people as Paul did, we want to be clear that the Gospel of Christ changes imperfect people over a period of time. In the meantime, this imperfection which we all have in common should not hold us back in our pursuit of God's best. Sometimes, the best counselors are those who have experienced the pain of life's circumstances, their own sin, and the consequences when others sins against them. The old adage "never trust a man without a limp" illustrates how God redeems our hurt and transforms it into a platform for personal ministry and disciple-making.

The Back Story of Philippians

Before we analyze the above verse more closely, it is important to understand Paul's exhortation to the Philippians leading up to chapter 3. Paul is in prison, and in chapter 1, after greeting his friends warmly and thanking God for them, Paul assures them that his imprisonment is for the good of the Gospel. Even in prison, Paul wants to help the Philippians think differently about how his confinement has served to enhance his love for Christ. Rethinking suffering is a key component in counseling.[19]

Paul counsels his friends to look at his suffering from a providential point of view so they may have peace knowing that God is in control and not distant. Paul further assures them that his love for God is strong and that their prayers have given him strength in Christ and His Spirit. It is this same Spirit that will give them strength to live in a manner worthy of the gospel of Christ.

In chapter 2, Paul starts by calling the Philippians to unity. If they strive to live lives worthy of the Gospel, it will be demonstrated in their pursuit of unity and love toward one another. Their supreme example in this is, of course, Christ Himself. If they will follow Him without complaint, they will be useful "lights" in a dark world. We cannot become like Christ if we are bogged down in our own immaturity and consumed with ourselves.

Built on this background, Paul enters chapter 3 ready to share himself. He has told them what they need to know and now he is ready to show them how to walk so that they can join him on the same road, reaching forward for the goal. Paul gets even more personal in chapter 3 when he shows us that there were factors in his past that, although he counts them as **"rubbish,"** have led him to an overwhelming appreciation of what is his **"in Christ."** Paul begins the chapter with a bold encouragement to **"rejoice in the Lord."** Within a dozen verses of this third chapter, Paul will make a strong case for the believer's cause to rejoice! **Finally, my brethren, rejoice in the Lord. To write the same things again is no trouble to me, and it is a safeguard for you. Beware of the dogs, beware of the evil workers, beware of the false circumcision** (Philippians 3:1-2).

In chapter 2, Paul had just given examples of God at work in the lives of Timothy and Epaphroditus, who were faithfully following Christ despite the hardships they encountered. In chapter 3, God uses those two men in the midst of challenges. Paul reminds his readers that they need to beware of a "present challenge" they will face. He

---

19 See *Curing the Heart* by Howard A. Eyrich and William L. Hines, Mentor Publishing, pages 117, 121-123 for a discussion on the need to rethink problems and apply a biblical point of view. See also Ch. 6 of this book for further study on the subject of the Christian mind.

warns of the source of this danger with three strong descriptions: **"dogs," "evil workers,"** and **"the false circumcision."** Each label is preceded by "beware." These are things that could lead them astray by false teaching. Paul gives a clue to his readers, in verse 3, of the dangerous teaching that comes from this group: **for we are the true circumcision, who worship in the Spirit of God and glory in Christ Jesus and put no confidence in the flesh** (Philippians 3:3).

They were apparently teaching that faith in Christ alone was not sufficient to achieve righteousness, which is contrary to the Gospel. False teachers were claiming that right standing before God must be achieved through works of the flesh. This is the perfect introduction to what Paul shares with his readers in verses 4, 5, and 6 of Philippians 3. Keep in mind the propensity within each of us to lean completely on our own strength, in order to overcome the things that estrange us from the fellowship we seek with God (see Proverbs 3:5-8). Paul is about to remind us that approaching God based on our own strength and pedigree is foolish indeed: **Although I myself might have confidence even in the flesh. If anyone else has a mind to put confidence in the flesh, I far more: circumcised the eighth day, of the nation of Israel, of the tribe of Benjamin, a Hebrew of Hebrews; as to the Law, a Pharisee; as to zeal, a persecutor of the church; as to the righteousness which is found in the Law, found blameless** (Philippians 3:4-6).

As if presenting a resume, Paul offers his credentials as one who might, mistakenly, be confident in his own ability to be right before God. The list includes all the impressive milestones in the life of an exemplary Jewish man. **"Circumcised the eighth day"** showed he had been raised from birth following distinct tradition. **"Of the nation of Israel, of the tribe of Benjamin, a Hebrew of Hebrews,"** indicates that his genealogy was pure and intact. If being a certified member of God's chosen people gave him an advantage when it came to being accepted by God, Paul had it! If right standing before God came from pursuing righteousness by following the Law, or by being recognized as a learned religious leader, or by zealously trying to stamp out any opposition to the religious system of the Pharisees, then Paul would be considered blameless in the eyes of the world. But here is where Paul makes the case with the truth of the Gospel that makes all the difference: **But whatever things were gain to me, those things I have counted as loss for the sake of Christ** (Philippians 3:7).

With these words, Paul begins the contrast that shows the weakness in the previous list of the attributes. People we counsel will often try to hold on to things in their past that, in light of God's truth, do not make sense. Paul recognizes there is no spiritual benefit from his efforts in the flesh. His efforts now are to press on to gain that which is truly valuable: **More than that, I count all things to be loss in view of the surpassing value of knowing Christ Jesus my Lord, for whom I have suffered the loss of all things, and count them but rubbish so that I may gain Christ, and may be found in Him, not having a righteousness of my own derived from the Law, but that which is through faith in Christ, the righteousness which comes from God on the basis of faith** (Philippians 3:8-9).

What is worth the loss of those attributes that Paul had held dear and that his religious world had admired? Paul states it plainly as **"knowing Jesus Christ my Lord."** With that phrase, Paul states his objective, focuses on his target, and reveals his destination. The false ideas of his former life all fell to the side when Paul set his sights on **"gaining Christ."** His desire to be **"found in Him"** was a process that came about not by Paul's own attempt at righteousness, but came from God **"on the basis of faith."** That is the key for anyone who would cease from the futile cycle of trying and failing. Paul is pointing out to his readers that God accepts us when we have the righteousness that comes from Him on the basis of faith in Christ: **that I may know Him and the power of His resurrection and the fellowship of His sufferings, being conformed to His death; in order that I may attain to the resurrection from the dead** (Philippians 3:10 -11).

Up to this point in chapter 3, Paul has instructed the believers that the notion of a relationship with God brought about through human efforts is wrong. In verses 10 and 11, Paul tells the Philippians that a relationship with God is to be experienced in the same way salvation occurs—through their faith in Christ. The salvation experience is rooted in real events in the past that have eternal significance. The new life in Christ is based upon faith that is dynamic, on-going, and something to be experienced. Paul is clear that we are to be spiritually involved and identified with the Savior. To really know Him, the power of His resurrection, and the fellowship of His sufferings is not only possible, but is expected because of our identity with Christ: **"being conformed to His death"** (Philippians 3:10).

106

Paul has told us that he wants to be as wholly conformed to Christ in his prison experience as possible. Yet he is not talking about manufacturing opportunities to suffer, for then it is not suffering for Christ; it is suffering because of one's own contrived behavior. Suffering for the will of God will come for His purposes in His time (1 Peter 4:12-19). *We are not to pursue suffering; we are to pursue Christ!* In the pursuit of Christ, we will know suffering (John 16:33). and our desire is to be like Him, even in suffering.

The Present Goal of Becoming Like Christ

Paul's aim for us is to be like Christ. To become like Him in His death may not sound like a pursuit, but remember it in the context of Romans 6. In Romans, Paul writes that we died and were raised with Christ. This means that when Christ died, we died to sin with Him in salvation. We who believe in Christ alone for eternal life have now died to sin in the sense that the wages for sin were paid in full. We no longer need to die again for our sins since Christ is our perfect sacrifice. Now, since we are raised with Him, we are raised to new life. In this earthly life, the reign of sin is broken and we are free to live by faith in obedience to Him by saying "no" to sin by the power of the Holy Spirit inside of us. Conforming to His death and attaining to the resurrection is the process of overcoming, by saying "No" to the old man with his selfish desires and saying "Yes" to the new man who is being changed to Christ-likeness.

Not that I have already obtained this or am already perfect, but I press on to make it my own, because Christ Jesus has made me his own (Philippians 3:12). This is one of those passages of Scripture that seems to leap off the page at us. One reason is that we see Paul's deep humility repeated from earlier verses. A second reason is that even though Paul is certain that he is new in Christ (2 Corinthians 5:17), and that his sin is forgiven (Romans 8:1), he knows that he has not spiritually and morally attained the things spoken of in verses 10 and 11 with the consistency that he will have when he meets his Savior face to face (1 Corinthians 13:12). Far from presenting anything close to sinless perfection in this life, Paul is letting us know that he is always in pursuit of maturity. The word used here in the ESV translated **"perfect"** is the same word translated in verse 15 as **"mature."** We will see this develop as we move along in the passage.

In his commitment to becoming conformed to the image of Christ, Paul **"presses on."** The term used is of vigorous, concentrated pursuit.[20] Paul is fixed with vigor on the goal of becoming what Christ wants him to become. But in the process of becoming like Christ, he is aware that the pursuit is not a pursuit of his own making. The language of the New American Standard Bible is helpful here: . . . **I press on so that I may lay hold of that for which also I was laid hold of by Christ Jesus** (Philippians 3:12b).

To lay hold of that for which I was laid hold of by Jesus Christ is a wonderful picture of the process of sanctification: that process by which we pursue the Lord as He works to grow us up in the Christian life. When my son was two years old, I used to raise him up, high off the ground so that he could feel the wind from our air conditioner blow through his hair. I grabbed him under his arms and as his speed accelerated from the floor, he grew excited and fearful all at once. In his journey of getting further off the ground, he grabbed my arms to hang on for the ride. I have often seen that as an example of what Paul is talking about here. Jesus grabs us for His purposes and we grab Him back and hang on for a journey we could not even imagine. Yet it promises to be one that is full of service and discovery; one that He always had in mind, and which is ours to experience in ever-increasing measure with Him all along the way (Ephesians 2:10).

Why does Christ lay hold of us? He lays hold of all of those who believe in Him for the same reason: His own glory. God does all things to glorify Himself (1 Corinthians 10:31; Ephesians 1:12, 14) and it glorifies Him when those who come to Him grow spiritually by becoming like Christ. It is to Christ-likeness that all Christians are called and that requires that we grow throughout our lives from less mature "babes" in Christ to more mature Christ followers. We point out three facets of this calling:

1. All Christians are called to the various commands and admonitions of Scripture. For example, we are to all seek peace and holiness (Hebrews 12:14) and the love of the brethren (John 13:34-35). Passages such as Colossians 3:12-17 show

---

20 Gramacki, Robert, *Philippians and Colossians: Joy and Completeness in Christ*, Mal Couch and Ed Hindson General Editors. (Chattanooga, AMG Publishers, 2003), p. 23.

Christians what character to exhibit toward one another in the Church as Ephesians 5:22-6:1 describes family relationships.

2. The Holy Spirit gives all Christians gifts and ministries in the church, and these differ among various believers (Romans 12; 1 Corinthians 12; Ephesians 12; 1 Peter 4). These gifts are to be used as works of service and for the building up of the church. Believers are called to exercise one or more of these gifts within the church body.

3. As we build on (1) our Christian character that develops as we faithfully obey Christ and, (2) our personal understanding of how the Holy Spirit has gifted each one of us for service, we are to serve Christ by becoming examples of Christ in the local church, the Church at large and in our own communities through the special ministries to which He leads us.

All three of these categories should be emphasized in biblical counseling and discipleship to encourage people that God has a real plan for the believer. Following His plan gives purpose and meaning and keeps us from falling into the darkness that blinds us to truth.

Why did Christ lay hold of you? First and foremost His reason is always for His own glory (1Corinthians 10:31). Second, He loves you. There are many aspects of His glory and love for us to discover as it is manifested over our lifetime. We are to stay in relationship with Him, always seeking Him through the twists and turns in the journey, as He leads us along the way. It must be kept in mind and constantly reinforced, that as our mind is renewed, we walk with Him in new ways, making new discoveries, and it is by this continued renewing of the mind that we are able to discover God's will (Romans 12:1-2). We know His will by being in His will. It is a problem when we have not followed Him for some time and then look for His will in a time of crisis. Walking with Him in righteousness makes His will easier to ascertain. Paul knew the value of always pressing on: **Brethren, I do not regard myself as having laid hold of it yet; but one thing I do: forgetting what lies behind and reaching forward to what lies ahead, I press on toward the goal for the prize of the upward call of God in Christ Jesus** (Philippians 3:13-14, NASB).

Paul's reference to the readers as "brothers" (**"brethren"**) harkens back to 1:12 and the opening verses of the epistle where Paul is so intimate. He wants to get their attention. Some imagine that he is concerned that they have been taught by some that they can reach perfection in this life.[21] Having gained their attention, he wants them to know that whatever they may think of themselves, they have not yet arrived. Have they surpassed the apostle in their experience? Surely not, and that is the point. Since no one has arrived at the goal, continuing in the pursuit of it is the only option (see Hebrews 12:1-2). The runner does not quit the race because it has become too difficult. But how does the Christian keep going when the goal seems difficult to attain? Here are three ways to press on:

1. Press on by forgetting what lies behind.[22]

Could you imagine a runner in a long distance race who is so concerned in mile three about the mistake he made in mile one that he turns around to go back and correct it? Of course, he would not do such a thing. He forgets about the mistake knowing that it is in the past. That is one reason we must take Paul's counsel seriously, and once we have brought our sin before the throne of grace in repentance we must understand that there is no condemnation for those who are in Christ Jesus (Romans 8:1). If God does not condemn me, I must not condemn myself. I do not need to "forgive myself," as modern thinking promotes, because only God can forgive me, since my sin is against Him (Psalm 51:4). I simply must agree that in Christ I am forgiven because He says so and not because of how I feel (1 John 1:9). Feelings will follow my line of thinking as I replace faulty thoughts with biblical truth from God's Word.

2. Press on by reaching or straining forward to what lies ahead.

For Paul, the picture is of one straining to reach something, not casually putting a hand out. To run with intensity requires a suitable goal. In the goal of the upward call of God, Christians are to run the race by focusing on Christ in all that they do. He is the finish line.

---

21 See *New Testament Commentary: Philippians, Colossians and Philemon* by William Hendriksen on Philippians 3:13, Baker Book House.

22 For a presentation on bringing the issues of the past into biblical focus see *Leaving Yesterday Behind: A Victim No More*, by William L. Hines, Christian Focus Publications.

It is easy to become discouraged if you do not know where you are going or lose sight of the goal and its importance. Loving God and becoming more like Christ is worth straining for and it will keep us moving forward as we nurture love for God and others in our hearts as a way of life (Mark 12:28-31).

3. <u>Press on by keeping in focus the prize of the upward call of God in Christ Jesus.</u>

The Prize of knowing God and His love, power, and forgiveness was awarded to us at the beginning of the Christian life when we first believed, and yet it is a call that is ongoing. This call of God represents a tension that continues to pull us Heavenward as we live in this world as citizens of Heaven (Philippians 3:20). This is the growing acknowledgement the Christian has that, although he lives in this world for a while longer, his attitudes and loyalties are best represented by the heavenly kingdom of Christ. It is this upward call that Paul is talking about and to which the Christian should always be adapting, by putting off of the attitudes of this world and putting on the attitudes of the Kingdom of God by the renewing of the mind (Ephesians 4:22-24). Perhaps it helps to think of yourself on a timeline toward Heaven. All along the line, there is the Spirit of God tugging your heart toward Heaven, yet there is what Paul calls the flesh pulling you back toward the earth. The Christian's responsibility is to say "No!" to the flesh and to continue reaching Heavenward.

Conclusion

Can we leave the past behind? Paul says we can, but not without consciously considering the past to be of no use and focusing on the prize of becoming like Christ. What marks a true Christian is not that he is without flaws, but that he leaves the past behind and grabs on to Christ, living for Him and if necessary dying for Him. Looking at each day as a new day to glorify God is the calling of every Christian. If we stumble we are to confess it and turn from our sin to follow Christ once again. He has called Christians to live in the present, looking toward the future. Both God and Paul want us to leave our past behind and . . . **press on to lay hold of that for which we have been laid hold of in Christ Jesus.**

PERSONAL CONNECTION QUESTIONS

Consider the following seriously. Make notes and write out plans to accomplish these things in your life for the glory of God. Use small cards you can carry with you throughout the day as a reminder of the principles to be considered and change to be accomplished.

1. What are those things in your past that hold you back? Is it sin for which you have not accepted God's forgiveness? Or maybe it is some past accomplishment that you had based your life upon, but God is telling you to look for new ways to please Him and new accomplishments to achieve by faith? Perhaps it is an unfulfilled expectation about which you have become bitter or spiritually paralyzed?

2. Have you truly recognized God's great mercy in laying hold of you by giving your life to Christ? Are you willing to lay hold of Him, whatever the cost and whatever the destination?

3. Meditate on this prayer of King David and make it your own:

> **Search me, O God, and know my heart!**
> **Try me and know my thoughts!**
> **And see if there be any grievous way in**
> **me, and lead me in the way everlasting**
> (Psalm 139:23-24).

Ask God to show you the grievous ways in you. Purposely acknowledge your sins and leave them at the cross. Follow His lead by seeking the things that draw you closer to Him.

4. Choose today to please Him in as many ways as possible. Don't rest on the laurels or failings of the past and don't wait for a bigger way to please Him in the future. The little things you do today honor Him and they lead to the big things of the future. These

things do not make you more "saved" or acceptable. They bring profound gladness to the Father's heart.

5. Choose to die for Him to the things of the flesh today so that you can live for Him tomorrow.

Notes

Chapter 10
PAUL AND RACE RELATIONS

Herbert Gooden, Deric Thomas and Bill Hines

For he himself is our peace, who has made us both one and has broken down in his flesh the dividing wall of hostility by abolishing the law of commandments expressed in ordinances, that he might create in himself one new man in place of the two, so making peace, and might reconcile us both to God in one body through the cross, thereby killing the hostility.
Ephesians 2:14-16

Paul tells the Ephesians that Jesus Christ made peace by sacrificing Himself. In every sense, Christ was their Peace and the basis of their being at peace with God. They were no longer enemies separated from God. The early Christians had faith in Christ, who had broken the walls that separated them from one another, despite radically different backgrounds. Believing Jews and believing Gentiles were now united in Christ. Paul explained to those in Ephesus that Christ fulfilled the Law of Moses since all of those commandments, ordinances, and rituals exposed the inability of sinful man to keep the law perfectly (Romans 3:19-20). Christ provided His Church a new covenant entirely for both Jews and Gentiles, making them one, at peace, and on an equal level by joining them in union in one faith family.

Through the Person, sacrifice, and mediation of Christ, sinners are allowed to draw near to God as a Father and are brought with acceptance into His presence with their worship under the teaching of the Holy Spirit as one with the Father and the Son. Christ purchased the right for us to approach God and the Spirit gives a new heart and strength to come by grace to serve God sufficiently well.

Sadly, if Paul were here today, he would find racial division within his immediate geographical area as well as everywhere around the world. Paul, who was a chosen vessel of God (Acts 9:15), acting as an empowered vessel of Christ with the gifts of the Spirit like the word of wisdom (1 Corinthians 1:7), word of knowledge

(2 Corinthians 2:14), faith (1 Corinthian 13:2), gifts of healing (Acts 14:9, 10), working of miracles (Acts 19:11), prophecy (1 Corinthian 13:2), and discerning of spirits (Acts 14:9) would be dismayed at the division among the body of Christ based upon race and cultural differences. Paul would be outraged at the racial divide and wall that exists not only in the world today but specifically in the church.

Jesus and the Samaritans

In the days of Jesus there was racism among tribes and clans. The racism between the Jews and the Samaritans was that of thinking of a people group as "unclean." (See John 8:48 where Jesus is referred to as a "Samaritan" in a derogatory manner).

The reason for thinking of the Samaritans as "unclean" and "foolish" could have to do with thinking of them unkindly as "half-breeds." After the siege of Sargon in 722 B.C. many of the Jews were taken away in captivity. Those left behind intermarried with foreigners from Babylon and surrounding territories who were brought in after the siege. To that mixed population was given the name *Samaritans* after Samaria. While this population believed itself to be of those who worship Yahweh, the true God, they were rejected as equal with the Jews and their hatred toward the Jews and Jerusalem grew. Having been rejected by the Jewish elite, the Samaritans built their own temple on Mt. Gerizim and continued an adulterated form of Judaism.

Remember how, in the story of the Good Samaritan, those who should have known better passed by the injured Jew? Yet a Samaritan whom they looked down upon was the one who showed kindness (Luke 10:30-36). Jesus told that parable because He is not concerned with the differences that man sees. In John 4 He demonstrates that with the Samaritan woman at the well. He simply sees a sinner in need of the Savior.

There are several things Jesus did in this account that show His awareness of the racial and ethnic problem and His answer to it. First, Jesus went through Samaria on His journey from Judea to Galilee. He could have gone around Samaria but He went through it. Not only did this demonstrate His openness to the Samaritan people but His recognition that He had a divine appointment at Jacob's. It was at this well that a woman came to Him in the day and He asked her for a drink of water. Speaking with a woman when alone was not something that was done, hence the surprise of the disciples when they returned from getting food in the nearby town. We see also from the woman's response that she was surprised at the request because, being a Samaritan, she would not expect a Jew to be friendly, let alone drink from the same vessel as she. In our own American culture this smacks of the days when Birmingham, Alabama's drinking fountains were marked *White* and *Colored*.

Note also in this account that Jesus entrusted to this Samaritan woman deep truths about Himself. His knowledge of the things of God was portrayed through His description of the new life in the Spirit He could give her. We also clearly see that this Rabbi, whom we know to be the Savior, was willing to demonstrate His omniscience in knowing about the husbands she had not yet spoken of and the future of worship for the people of God. But then we see the greatest revelation of all: Jesus clearly communicates to her that He is the Messiah that the entire world waits for, not just the Samaritans or the Jews. When the people of the region in His day would have easily passed the Samaritan woman by or possibly insulted her or perhaps offered a cordial but distant nod of the head, Jesus did not. Jesus fully engaged her as one for whom He came.

Many of us who are baby boomers remember the civil rights marches and the animosity of those times. Even some in the Church were in favor of segregation. Some would help a black or Hispanic Church financially yet did not want those of another race attending their white church. Jesus is no bigot. Not toward women or ethnicities not His own. His insight and compassion looks at the heart and its needs and gifts, not at the outward appearance. Jesus lived this out as we saw His kindness toward the woman at the well, and He lived it toward people such as the Roman Centurion whose servant was ill (Mathew 8:5-13).[23] God showed throughout Scripture that many were invited to the kingdom of God, some through the most intimate of human relationships.

---

23 Note in this passage that many will sit at the feast in the kingdom from other lands, while those who consider themselves of the kingdom of Abraham will be thrown out.

Race and Marriage[24]

As counselors and people-helpers we may be asked to comment as to whether it is proper to marry outside of one's race. We must be united on this: If the marriage between two individuals meets biblical requirements for marriage, then race is not an issue. We should, of course, discuss possible difficulties of interracial marriage as we would discuss the difficulties of marriage across economic or cultural boundaries, but race is a challenge to be understood; not a reason to prohibit the marriage union in Christ. Recall the account of Boaz and Ruth (Ruth 4:13-22, Matthew 1:31). A Moabite married a Jew and it was blessed of God. It was their union that produced Obed, the father of Jesse, who was the father of King David, on whose throne would one day sit One born of his lineage, Jesus the Messiah (Mathew 1:1, 8; Luke 3:31).

The Bible does forbid the marriage of a believer and an unbeliever. "A wife is bound to her husband as long as he lives. But if her husband dies, she is free to be married to whom she wishes, only in the Lord" (1 Corinthians 7:39). The phrase, "in the Lord" means that both man and woman must be Christians. It is the same idea put forth through Moses in Deuteronomy 7:3-4: **You shall not intermarry with them [people from other nations who are unbelievers], giving your daughters to their sons or taking their daughters for your sons, for they would turn away your sons from following me, to serve other gods. Then the anger of the Lord would be kindled against you, and he would destroy you quickly.** The issue is not marrying those of other nations, per se, but marrying those who do not worship the God of the Bible.

John Piper makes four observations concerning interracial marriage in Chapter 15 of his book, *Bloodlines: Race, Cross, and the Christian which are* worth mentioning here: [25]

1. All races have one ancestor in the image of God, and all humans are in God's image.

---

24 See *Bloodlines: Race, Cross, and the Christian* by John Piper, chapter 15 for an excellent discussion of interracial marriage. Many ideas from that chapter are included here.
25 *Bloodlines: Race, Cross, and the Christian*, p. 212

2. The Bible forbids intermarriage between unbeliever and believer, but not between races.

3. In Christ, our oneness is profound and transforms racial and social differences from barriers to blessings.

4. Criticizing one interracial marriage was severely disciplined by God (see Numbers 12:1-10).

In the context of this chapter, "the issue is not that of color mixing, or customs mixing, or clan identity. The real issue is: *will there be one common allegiance to the true God in this marriage or will there be divided affections?*"[26]

Christians are called to love one another in the Spirit as Christ loves us (John 13:34-35). With generations of cultural bias is such unity possible? God says that not only is it possible, it is commanded. Let us delve deeper into the unity of the Spirit of God working in brothers and sisters in Christ.

United in God: True Identity as it Relates to Race

In the beginning, God's creation was "good," meaning "pure" with no "bad" in it. It was uncorrupted. God created every kind of animal and plant to reproduce after its own kind (Genesis 1:12; 25). In fact, the phrase "after their kind" appears ten times in Genesis 1. The implication is that each kind will produce its own kind.[27]

Like the plants and animals, God made man. Unlike the plants and animals, God made man in His own image (Genesis 1:26). God made man as one race, the human race with genetic variability in DNA possible to produce a great number of different combinations of such things as hair, eye, and *skin* color. These differences are only a very small percentage of our genetic variability but for those who look at the outward appearance, skin color variations are a dividing line that they mistakenly believe produces many "races." God warned Samuel in 1 Samuel 16:7 about evaluating a person based upon outward appearance alone in the selection of a new king for Israel: **But the Lord said to Samuel, "Do not look on his appearance**

---

26 Piper, John, *Bloodlines: Race, Cross, and the Christian*, p. 210.
27 Ham, Ken & A. Charles Ware. *One Race One Blood*, pp.102,107. Master Books, 2007.

or on the height of his stature, because I have rejected him. For the Lord sees not as man sees: man looks on the outward appearance, but the Lord looks on the heart."

Good biblical counselors understand that there is only one race and that the differences in skin color and the like are simply variations within the one race. Starting a counselee at the beginning of man's creation by God, found in the book of Genesis, is crucial for anyone who does not understand who they are and, more importantly, who their Creator is. The guided tour through Genesis will show how God created man in His own image and likeness[28] and created him to have dominion over all that had been created. God blessed the man and woman and said in Genesis 1:28a: "Be fruitful and multiply, and replenish the earth and subdue it." God assigns responsibilities to man as a sign of His own nature. God's creation of mankind in His very own image endowed man with capacities beyond animals, such as a mind, a will, and a soul (Genesis

Unlike animals, mankind can be united in relationships and especially in marriage in order to reflect the glory of God. Psalm 133:1 states: **Behold, how good and pleasant it is when brothers dwell in unity!** In particular, God instituted marriage, unique to mankind, as the union of one man and one woman. In the first marriage, God performed the ceremony and the response of Adam is recorded in Genesis 2:23-25: **Then the man said, "This at last is bone of my bones and flesh of my flesh; she shall be called Woman, because she was taken out of Man." Therefore a man shall leave his father and his mother and hold fast to his wife, and they shall become one flesh. And the man and his wife were both naked and were not ashamed.** In Genesis 2:25, the Word reveals that the man and his wife experienced true intimacy and unveiled communication with one another. They saw each other as God sees. There was no danger of looking at the body as an object, separate from the person.[29] They had not sinned and there was no shame. Life was "good," meaning "pure" and "perfect," as the human race started with simply the first two created people. We also observe that in the creation passage of Genesis God does not tell us the color of the skin of Adam and Eve.

---

28 Heart: your inner, spiritual person consisting of your mind, spirit and soul. Shaw, Mark, *The Heart of Addiction: A Biblical Perspective*, (Bemidji, MN, Focus Publishing, 2008).

29 Healy, Mary, *Men and Women are from Eden*, Servant Books, 2005, p. 27.

Divided by Sin: Distorted Identity as it Relates to Race

So how has mankind forgotten his original identity in creation as it relates to race? The answer is simple: the first man, Adam, along with Eve, sinned, and the consequence from their sin is the depravity of mankind (Genesis 5:3; 6:5). Each person is now born with a sinful nature. Left alone, each person will choose to walk away from God in pursuit of pleasing oneself.

Adam and Eve were perfect and had a perfect genetic make-up until their own sinful choices corrupted the entire world.[30]Tempted and deceived by Satan in the Garden of Eden, Adam and Eve immediately experienced spiritual death, separation from God, suffering, and sadness as a result of their disobedience of God's Word.

Though there are many people groups and cultural differences in the nations around the world, we all are children of Adam and Eve and "fallen" in our nature—desperate sinners needing a Savior. No matter what language a person speaks, no matter what skin color a person has been given, and no matter where a person lives, each person must be born again (John 3:3). Everyone is united in their lost state and in need of Christ!

Racism today stems from a distorted view of God and His creation. Prejudices are generated by one's sinful, divisive nature in the heart. Unless truly born again by the Spirit of God, a person will not see others through the biblical lens as united as one race.[31]Like all of us, the Apostle Paul was once a divisive, racist person who persecuted Christians until he met the Lord Jesus Christ.

United in Christ: Restoration of True identity as it Relates to Race

Only one thing can unite all people groups: the blood of Christ. The Apostle Paul suffered in his past from extreme ethnocentrism[32]as

---

30 Ken, Ham & A. Charles Ware, *One Race One Blood*, pp. 102,107.

31 Suggested term used for the identification of the human kind. We are all Homo sapiens. More and more scientists find the differences that set us apart are cultural and not racial. Ibid,112-114.

32 The conviction or feeling that one's own ethnic group should be treated as a superior or privileged. Piper, John, *Blood Lines: Race, Cross, and the Christian*, p.115.

the chief persecutor of Christians (Acts 7:58; 8:1; 9:1; 22:4). As an educated man and a member of the Jewish faith, Paul had been blind to the truth of Jesus' gospel of the kingdom. He was actively involved in attacking the disciples of Christ, breaking up meetings, burning their books, and bringing women and men to trial. He hated those he perceived as different and inferior to him until he was confronted and blinded by Jesus Christ on the journey to Damascus (Acts 1:1-19). In Damascus, Paul was filled with the Holy Spirit and healed of his literal and spiritual blindness. He then began to preach Christ.

A focus upon anything else other than Christ will only lead to division. True intimacy and unity can only be restored through the Person and work of Christ. Personal agendas and preferences only lead to division. Likewise, a focus upon skin color and other minor genetic and cultural differences will only lead to division. Diversity is a blessing, not a curse, and unity is possible despite the infinite variability of God's human creations.

Skilled biblical counselors addressing prejudicial issues of all kinds, as well as racial tension, will ask probing questions like these to help discern sinful and erroneous thinking that does not align with the Word of God:

- Has a bad experience with one person led you to be prejudiced against an entire group of people?

- Have stereotypes of a certain group led you to prejudices against an entire group?

- Do you see people as possessors of souls made in God's image or merely as objects?

- Have negative images in the media of a particular group of people influenced your opinion against them?

- Has peer pressure or parental influence persuaded you to adopt an intolerant attitude against a certain person or group?

- Has the color of a person's skin led you to be prejudiced against an entire group?

- Has a misunderstanding of cultural values led to prejudices toward a particular group?

- Has belief in evolution led you to believe that humans have evolved rather than being created in the image of God?

- Do you think of humans as one race?

- Do you think some people groups are superior to others?

Answers that differ from the Word of God to any of these questions enable a biblical counselor to discover the spiritual blindness and divisive walls that the counselee has erected.

United in the Church: Division by Race Abolished

The Apostle Paul emphasized the importance of unity of those in the local faith family (Ephesians 4:1-7). The church finds unity in the blood of Christ, according to Ephesians 2:13: **But now in Christ Jesus you who once were far off have been brought near by the blood of Christ.** Today, true worship of the One True God is not the source of division. Instead, Christians choose to separate themselves denominationally by every imaginable peripheral doctrine and personal preference, such as types of music and the like. In some places in America, Christians are divided simply because of skin color and cultural differences in worship style.

Why the division? The simple answer is that church has become a place of personal preference and a place to meet people's needs rather than a place to worship God. Christians fail to fight for unity with one another, which Paul says is vital in Ephesians 4:1-7: **"I therefore, a prisoner for the Lord, urge you to walk in a manner worthy of the calling to which you have been called, with all humility and gentleness, with patience, bearing with one another in love, eager to maintain the unity of the Spirit in the bond of peace. There is one body and one Spirit, just as you were called to the one hope that belongs to your call one Lord, one faith, one baptism, one God and Father of all, who is over all and through all and in all. But grace was given to each one of us according to the measure of Christ's gift."**

Christ came and preached peace, that we are no longer strangers and foreigners, but fellow citizens with other believers in the household of God (Ephesians 2:19). It is why we call each other "brother" and "sister," since we have the same Heavenly Father and live in the same household of faith!

The apostles and the prophets laid the foundation of Christianity for Christ-followers today. All believers, being united by faith and unconditional love, become a reflection of Jesus as His body. The church's actions in the world are a visible presentation of Christ to a lost and dying world. God dwells in mankind as they live in union with Him through the operation of his Spirit. United with Christ, we believe the same doctrine, worship the same God, practice the same holiness, and look forward to the same Heaven, regardless of our skin color and other minor genetic differences. On those things in which we disagree God will lead the maturing Christian unto greater maturity (Philippians 3:15-16).

United for Eternity: Eternal Identity as it Relates to Race

Heaven is not a place limited to one certain people group, one language, or one skin color. Heaven is a place limited to those who are trusting in Christ by grace alone. The unity believers demonstrate here on earth by being self-sacrificing, tolerant, and loving towards different people groups[33] is our preparation for when we meet our Savior once again in eternity with God in Heaven (Revelations 5:9). In Ephesians 4:20-24, Paul instructs Christians to put off the old self and with it *prejudices*[34] and practices of sin. Believers are to put on the new self that is being renewed in knowledge after the image of its creator (Colossians 3:9b-10). By the Holy Spirit's power, these new put on behaviors will produce in and through the Christian the following fruit of the Spirit: **love, joy, peace, patience, gentleness, goodness, faith, meekness, and self-control (**Galatians 5:22-23). Living with one another in unity and producing this type of fruit allows the believer to experience a foretaste of Heaven, though it will pale in comparison to the actual place.

---

33 Suggested term used for identification of the human kind. We are all Homo sapiens. More and more scientist find the differences that set us apart are cultural not racial.

34 Ham, Ken & A. Charles Ware, *One Race One Blood* , p. 112-114.

The book of The Revelation of Jesus Christ paints the reality of unity that all believers will one day experience for eternity: **After this I looked, and behold, a great multitude that no one could number, from every nation, from all tribes and peoples and languages, standing before the throne and before the Lamb, clothed in white robes, with palm branches in their hands, and crying out with a loud voice, "Salvation belongs to our God who sits on the throne, and to the Lamb!" And all the angels were standing around the throne and around the elders and the four living creatures, and they fell on their faces before the throne and worshiped God, saying, "Amen! Blessing and glory and wisdom and thanksgiving and honor and power and might be to our God forever and ever! Amen"** (Revelation 7:9-12).

PERSONAL CONNECTION QUESTIONS

1. When you see a person of a different ethnicity, what are the first thoughts that come to your mind? When the next opportunity arises, introduce yourself to a same gender person from a different ethnic group to strike up a conversation with him/her. Afterward, journal your experience.

2. Make a list of some of your fears regarding other people groups different from yours. Because 1 John 4:18b says **perfect love casts out fear,** list ways that you can demonstrate the perfect love of God to someone from a different cultural group from you. Pick out one person, or family, to serve in a Christ-like manner.

3. Pray about how you might serve Christ in another part of the world. How important is mission work to you? How can you use your skills to serve hurting and lost people around the world?

4. Action Assignment: Visit a Bible study group or church congregation with a different ethnic group from yours. Even if you do not speak the language, attend the service and participate in worshiping God your Creator together with them!

Chapter 11
PAUL AND WOMEN IN MINISTRY

Ruth Froese and Shirley Crowder

But as for you, teach what accords with sound doctrine. Older men are to be sober-minded, dignified, self-controlled, sound in faith, in love, and in steadfastness. Older women likewise are to be reverent in behavior, not slanderers or slaves to much wine. They are to teach what is good, and so train the young women to love their husbands and children, to be self-controlled, pure, working at home, kind, and submissive to their own husbands, that the word of God may not be reviled
Titus 2:1-5

Marvel at how Paul the Counselor equips women for a counseling ministry in these words above! Through God's Spirit, Paul outlines how women who live in the joy of Jesus Christ radiate God's plan for them. Paul proves an excellent counselor and instructor for future counselors. He spells out purpose and motivation, and addresses specific problematic issues with laser precision and beautiful relevance to every culture. As women embrace God's amazing design, their lives are characterized by delight, great dignity, and tremendous meaning.

Equality in Complementary Roles

Paul always believed in equality of personhood for men and women, which is evident when, as a young man, he was busy persecuting Christians, persecuting both genders equally (Acts 9:2). But then Paul meets Jesus Christ, and he is forever changed. Instead of continuing to lump Christian men and women together, his view of women gains a wonderful new dimension. Wise biblical counselors will stress Paul's teachings regarding women to those they are privileged to serve for the sole purpose of glorifying Christ alone.

While carefully reinforcing that men and women are equal in personhood, the Holy Spirit leads Paul to clearly emphasize differences in function.[35]Men and women are equal in deadness, apart from Jesus Christ (Ephesians 2:1-3); equal recipients of lavished grace, in Christ (Ephesians 2:4-10); equal heirs to an amazing inheritance, in God's family (Galatians 3:26-29); and, wonderfully, men and women have equally important but distinctive roles. This concept is often described by the word *complementarian.* The complementarian position affirms ". . . that God created man and woman equal in value and personhood, and equal in bearing his image, but that both creation and redemption indicate some distinct roles for men and women in marriage and in the Church."[36]Later in this chapter, practical aspects of the complementarian position will be explored.

But first, why is it important for women ministering as biblical counselors to agree with Paul about role differences? God tells us in Titus 2:5 that biblical womanhood holds the Word of God high by lives that shine with the gospel of Jesus Christ. If counselors neglect the practical aspects of biblical womanhood, they promote rebellion or apathy and, in effect, push women away from Christ. If counselors ignore the big picture of motivation and purpose, wrong conclusions are easily drawn. Tragically, many find false comfort in extra-biblical rules or become entrenched in rebellious refusal to embrace biblical roles. God's priorities counter such legalistic or feministic tactics. God's priorities draw women to cling to Christ Jesus in desperate dependence, and to live in sweet union with Jesus evidenced by victoriously reflecting His beautiful character.

Satan is working hard to denigrate role differences. Why? Because biblical womanhood has cosmic significance! Biblical womanhood shows off God's wisdom to angels and demons! In Ephesians 3, Paul writes that through the church **the manifold wisdom of God might now be made known to the rulers and authorities in the Heavenly places** (Ephesians 3:10). How on earth can the church impress the cosmic host? One of the first practical ways Paul lists is a wife submitting to her husband (Ephesians 5:22-24). In 1 Corinthians 11, Paul points to women as key players on the celestial stage. There he teaches the Corinthian women to fall under

---

35 1 Corinthians 11:1-16, 14:33-35, Ephesians 5:22-33, Colossians 3:18-19, 1 Timothy 2:9-15, Titus 2:1-8, 1 Peter 3:1-8.

36 Grudem, Wayne, *Systematic Theology*, p. 16, Zondervan.

the authority of male leaders in the church **because of the angels.** As women agree with God about authority in the church and home, they are cheered on by a galactic audience. In Isaiah 43:6-7, God says that all humans, sons and daughters, are created **for my glory.** When women embrace their biblical role, God's glory is seen on this planet and far beyond. What an incredible opportunity! With this in view it is easy to see why Satan is so pleased when feminism furthers the lie that complementarianism limits women in scope of opportunity.

As well as the cosmic shining observed by angels and demons, when women embrace God's plan for their lives, God is glorified here on earth. Titus 2:3-5 explains how women can live so **that the word of God may not be reviled.** Paul intensely desired to promote the Word of God. His urgent, clear, concise commands to women lay out practical ways they can provide a gospel signpost to the watching world. Women who long to love, obey, promote, and honor Jesus Christ receive Paul's counsel with gratitude and gladness and will impart these same truths to others, especially female counselees.

The Women in Paul's Ministry

Let's take a quick look at some of the women who served alongside Paul in ministry. God created women to be supportive, responsive, and nurturing, and these women provide examples in the flesh.

Women who provided a welcoming home where the Word of God was spoken:

- Lydia of Thyatira was a woman of prayer and hospitality (Acts 16:14-15).

- The four unmarried daughters of Philip the evangelist in Caesarea provided extended housing for Paul in their home, during which time they also prophesied (Acts 21:8). (Maybe they were the first female biblical counselors!)

- Prisca, or Priscilla, with her husband Aquilla, hosted an early church in their home. They were so grounded in the Word that when Apollos, a dynamic speaker, was off-base, **they took him and explained to him the way of God more accurately** (Acts 18:26).

Women with a helpful, responsive spirit:

- Phoebe of Cenchrea served **as a patron of many and of myself as well.** She is described as one who ran the errands or executed the commands of another (Romans 16:1).

- Prisca is named with her husband as friends who **risked their necks** for Paul's life (Acts 21:8).

- Mary **worked hard** for the church in Rome (Acts 18:26).

- Tryphena and Tryphosa were **workers in the Lord** (Romans 16:1).

- Euodia and Syntyche labored with Paul (Philippians 4:2).

- Junia, together with husband Andronicus, was a fellow prisoner with Paul. As early believers, they were also well known to the apostles (Romans 16:7).

- Chloe and her household assisted Paul in understanding the spiritual needs of the church at Corinth (1 Corinthians 1:11).

Women who nurtured:

- Eunice and her mother Lois, women of **sincere faith,** trained son and grandson Timothy in that faith (2 Timothy 1:5, 3:15).

- Rufus became like a mother to Paul (Romans 16:13).

These women are shining examples of the wisdom of God in creating women for His own glory and purposes.

Two Questions Answered by Paul

The background for Paul's commands in Scripture regarding women can be answered in two questions. The first question is: "Can we learn anything about biblical womanhood from God's perfect creation, before it was cursed by sin?" Paul refers to creation:

- In calling women to respect male headship in church and home (1 Corinthians 11:8-9).

- In calling women to follow male leadership in church and home (1 Timothy 2:11-14).

- In calling for marriages that imitate the marriage between Christ and the church (Ephesians 5:23-32).

In a manner similar to Christ, Paul defends his teaching by looking back to creation (Matthew 19:4-6). Likewise, counselors imitate Christ when they motivate counselees on the basis of creation perfection. These (and other) creation lessons regarding the role of a woman are confirmed through Paul's teaching on biblical womanhood, for those who love God and live in Christ:

- God gave man the job of naming (Genesis 2:19). The name-giver has authority over the named one. In Christ, women will have an agreeable or willing spirit toward authority (Ephesians 5:22-24, 33).

- Man was formed of dust from the ground outside the garden (Genesis 2:7-8). Woman was made from the rib of a man and created for man (Genesis 2:20-22). In Christ, women embrace this creation order by welcoming the protection and the priorities of appropriate men (1 Corinthians 11:9).

- Adam called himself "iysh," which means strong and manly, and he named Eve "ishshah," which means the opposite—soft and womanly (Genesis 2:23).[37]The very meaning of these names guides us in understanding role differences. In Christ, women love to portray soft womanliness (1Timothy 2:9-11; 1 Peter 3:3-4).

- Man was created outside the garden in Eden, and then put into it (Genesis 2:8). Woman was created in the garden, in the home where God had put her husband. In Christ, women don't incline themselves away from home; rather they devote themselves gladly to creating an oasis of calm and shelter (Proverbs 31, Titus 2:5).

- Man was given the command to tend, keep, and protect the garden from sin (Genesis 2:15-17). Woman was created for man, to help him and provide companionship (Genesis 2:18). In Christ, women are supportive, in respectful submission to their husband, if married (Ephesians 5:33; Colossians 3:18).

- Eve was deceived by the serpent (Genesis 3:1-4). In Christ,

---

37 Kassian, Mary & DeMoss, Nancy Leigh, *True Woman 101: Divine Design*, (Chicago, IL, Moody Publishers, 2012), p. 30.

women are alert about desires that make it easy to be deceived, such as the desire to control. They are teachable and leadable by their own husband and by godly male leaders in the church (2 Timothy 3:6-7; 1 Corinthians 14:33-35).

The second question Paul addresses is: "Since we are created in the image of God as His image bearers, does His character reveal anything about roles?" The Almighty Holy Father must, by nature of His holiness, condemn all sin and sinners. He sent His Servant Savior Son to bear this cross. Jesus submitted to His slaughter, achieving the Father's goal of redeeming mankind from the result of their sin. Jesus asked the Father to send His Holy Spirit to convict and comfort and help redeemed sinners until His return, when He gathers them as His glorious bride. Note the distinct and uncrossed role differences between Father, Son, and Spirit. Paul explains how role differences reflect the image of God when he writes **. . . the head of a wife is her husband, and the head of Christ is God** (1 Corinthians 11:3).

- Women imitate Christ when they embrace the role of nurturing through creating a welcoming home (Titus 2:5; Proverbs 31; John 14:3). Christ is presently preparing a home (John 14:2). Whether married or single, a woman can provide a little taste of Heaven as she nurtures those who live in or visit her home.

- Christ is **gentle and humble in heart** (Matthew 11:29, HCSB). Women imitate Christ by a gentle and quiet spirit in the face of others' sinful shortcomings (1 Peter 3:3-4).

- Women imitate Christ when they love their husband, which shows up in submission (Titus 2:4-5). As stated so well by Susan Hunt, "It defies logic that Jesus would release all the glories of Heaven so He could give us the glory of Heaven. Submission is not about logic; it is about love. Jesus loved us so much that He voluntarily submitted to death on a cross. His command is that wives are to submit to their husbands. It is a gift that we voluntarily give to the man we have vowed to love in obedience to the Savior we love".[38]

- Women imitate Christ when they fall under authority. Jesus didn't say or do anything apart from the Father's authority (John 5:19; 8:28-29). "If women want to fulfill God's purposes

---

38 Hunt, Susan, *The True Woman: The Beauty and Strength of a Godly Woman*, (Wheaton, Ill., Crossway, 1997), pp. 106-107.

for their lives they must be willing to relinquish control and allow God to lead through the men He's placed in positions of authority."[39]

As a biblical counselor, reminding women of these truths related to God their Creator is vital for living out God's wisdom in everyday life.

General Instruction for Women's Ministry

With eyes fixed on Christ, with whom we have been crucified (Galatians 2:20), and in whom we are hidden, look at the instructions Paul gave to women in ministry. In 1 Timothy 3:15 Paul said he was writing so that the church may know how one ought to behave in the household of God, which is the church of the living God, a pillar and buttress of truth. Paul's instructions to Titus in that book of the Bible address women in the organization of the local church. He emphasizes the importance of church leaders teaching sound doctrine (Titus 2:1), thus framing the context of spiritual authority under which all disciple-making occurs, and women minister as biblical counselors and disciple-makers. "When we respond humbly to male leadership in our homes and churches, we demonstrate a noble submission to authority that reflects Christ's submission to God His Father."[40]

In Titus 2, Paul gives instructions to specific groups in the church: older men, older women, younger men and slaves. As you read these instructions remember that "God did not design the Christian life to be lived independently. . . God intends for the lives of the people in the church to interweave, to influence each other and by these interactions to testify of the truth, power, and hope of the gospel."[41]

Paul sets the teaching priority within the church by the pastor equipping the older—spiritually mature—women to teach, disciple, admonish and encourage the younger women so that the Word of God may not be dishonored (Titus 2:5). Paul is saying that there are certain things that identify women as leaders and disciple-makers.

---

39 DeMoss, Nancy Leigh, *Becoming God's True Woman*, (Greenville, SC, Cross-way Books, 2002), p. 73.
40 "True Woman Manifesto": www.truewoman.com.
41 Ibid.

They have relationships and characteristics built on sound doctrine that enables them to live out their day-to-day lives in a way that glorifies God.

In 1 Peter 3:1-6 we learn about holy women. Holy women who hoped in God understood that God alone was their source of strength and that they were set apart from the world for service to the Lord. As a result, their manner and appearance brought glory to God as they adorned themselves with a gentle and quiet spirit,[42]leading them to be submissive to their husbands.

From the things Paul instructs older women to model and teach younger—spiritually immature—women, we find what qualifies one as an older woman and we gain an understanding of the qualifications of a woman biblical counselor. She is to:

- Be reverent in behavior

- Control her tongue

- Be free of life-dominating sins

1 Timothy 2:9-15 gives insight into what it means to be reverent in behavior. Paul tells women that their dress, attitude, and appearance are to be a reflection of their righteousness. They must behave and dress in a manner that does not diminish their testimony, but is a shining demonstration of God's grace that points to the Gospel of Christ. As she relates to the men whom God has placed in positions of spiritual authority over her in the church and home, she is respectful, submissive, gracious and humble. Reverent behavior is what 1 Peter 2:18 references when we read that unbelieving husbands can be won without a word. They are won by the behavior of their wives or the way their wives live godly and righteous lives.

Paul tells us that women must control their tongues. They are not to slander, gossip, argue, criticize or nag. Since we know that from **out of the abundance of the heart the mouth speaks** (Matthew 12:34), we understand that we can only speak loving, merciful, gracious, gentle, kind and encouraging words when we are being

---

42 The point about adorning is that you do not get caught up in the outward appearance, ie, make-up, hair styles, jewelry, clothing and shoes; and, that your outward appearance is God-glorifying.

diligent, by God's grace, to live godly and righteous lives that glorify God. How important this quality is for a woman skilled in biblical counseling!

When Paul tells us that an older woman **is not addicted to much wine** he is saying that she is not a lover of pleasure (2 Timothy 3:4), is **sober-minded** (2 Timothy 4 and 1 Peter 1:13), and is free of life-dominating sins. Life-dominating sins are behaviors that are excessive or that "take control" of our lives. Some of the areas in which women may find themselves struggling to overcome life-dominating sins are alcohol, drugs, pornography, gossip, illicit sexual behavior, various forms of witchcraft and sorcery, shopping, television, internet games or surfing, social media, and talking on the phone. A woman's obedient walk with the Lord in these areas will both bless her and display a godly example for those she counsels.

Specific Instruction for Women's Ministry

These days thousands of counselors tackle the problem of how best to provide help for women. A quick glance at the psychological research reveals a confusing array of treatments—cognitive therapy, family systems therapy, pharmacological therapy—to name a few.[43] Paul the counselor provides the best advice, after all he was inspired by the Holy Spirit. His forthright style is clear, direct and easily understood, imitating Jesus, whose pinpoint specificity targeted deep into every heart. As well, Paul's writings that specifically address women deal with many situations in numerous locations and occasions.

In Philippians 4:2-8 Paul pleads with Euodia and Syntyche, two influential women in the church who ministered **side by side** with Paul, Clement and **the rest of (Paul's) fellow workers,** to **agree in the Lord,** which means to be **of the same mind, having the same love, being in full accord and of one mind** (Philippians 2:2). He goes on to describe what he means by encouraging these women to be reasonable and to not be anxious (or in other words, to trust God).

As we think about all the things we are to be (reverent in behavior, able to control our tongues, free of life-dominating sins, reasonable, not anxious), we need to look at Paul's specific instructions

---

43 Hughes, R. Kent and Bryan Chapell, *1-2 Timothy and Titus: To Guard the Deposit,* (Wheaton, Ill, Crossway, 2012), pp. 355-356.

or counsel on HOW we can live out and teach those whom we counsel or disciple. Biblical counselors are to teach counselees the ideas set forth in Romans 12:1-2, 2 Timothy 1:13-15 and 1 Peter 4:13-15. We must teach counselees to not be conformed to this world and its trappings but be a living sacrifice to God and be holy in all (our) conduct by preparing (our) minds for action and being transformed by the renewal of (our) minds as we are diligent to be doers of the word. We are to teach them to be women of prayer and supplication so that the peace of God which surpasses all understanding will guard (our) hearts and minds in Christ Jesus which results in them trusting God.

Paul's counsel to women in Titus 2:3-5 is particularly appropriate for today's busy lifestyles and full agendas. He hits the "personal agenda" nail on the head by dealing with two types of priority structures. He prioritizes who is to provide counsel, which we've already looked at, and then he prioritizes what is to be counseled. Now if you're single, just hang on. Don't close this chapter yet. The content of Paul's counsel provides solutions for all kinds of women's problems, such as depression.

What was the first quality Paul listed that qualified a woman to counsel? Reverence. Respect for authority. In our culture, the problem of authority is in a way a bigger crisis than the crisis of truth.[44] Postmodern culture is a system that undermines authority. People often place themselves in the seat of judgment over authority. But God is a Judge to whom all are accountable, and without some recognition of authority, there is no place in their minds for the gospel. Look again at Titus 2:5, and note how Paul concludes the teaching toward women. Reverence for authority is the first requirement for teaching, so that the word of God may not be reviled. A woman must welcome and respect authority—God, the government, employers, the Church's elders, her husband – in order to bring glory to God and avoid disgrace of the Gospel in public and turmoil within her own heart.

---

44 Single women can live and apply the principle of submission to your spiritual authority where Paul speaks of being submissive to your husband.

The Content of Counsel

Paul teaches a simple three-part priority structure for married women. In Christ, women will embrace this cosmically impressive order of priority that holds the gospel high – whether single or married.

1. Love your husband. He must be his wife's number one priority and he must know it.

2. Love your children.[45] Mothers may not elevate their children above their husband!

3. Keep your home. This comes after husband and children, and before jobs and hobbies.

Sometimes women ask, "Where does God, or His church, fit in to that priority list?" Good question! God's prioritizing of a woman's life can only happen in union with Christ, and it happens as part of His body, the church, (Ephesians 4:1-5:24). Apart from union with Christ, which leads to reflecting His righteousness, women choose the curse of Genesis 3:16. Thus, children are elevated to a level of importance God never intended for them, and women desire to rule over their husband. And thus, self-definitions of righteousness abound, which Paul the Counselor would call deception (2 Timothy 6:5-7; 1 Timothy 2:14).

As well as the priority structure of God's ordering, Paul lists four qualifiers for how women are to live—with self-control, purity, kindness, submission. Each of these character qualities will be evidenced in a woman who reflects Christ, whether single or married. This is not because a woman has any righteousness of her own; rather it is because she is progressively growing in Christ's imputed righteousness.

The concept of self-control can mean discretion, good sense, prudence, graciousness, and good judgment.[46] We'll consider it in two areas: emotions and finances.

---

45 Single women, don't miss the idea that you are a "spiritual mother" to those whom you disciple.

46 See also the discussion of "self-control" in *New Testament Commentary: Galatians and Ephesians*, by William Hendriksen, p. 225. Baker Book House.

Writing while imprisoned, Paul commanded rejoicing, which produces the fruit of the Spirit called "joy" (Philippians 4:4; Galatians 5:22). Joy is not gushy happiness, but a byproduct of the Holy Spirit when a person has an inner intellectual state of mind focused upon the salvation and lordship of Jesus Christ. That's serious business these days, where women are given every justification to be moody. "Oh, you're in your cycle. That's OK, go ahead and bite your husband's head off. You must be getting your period." We must not buy in to that kind of thinking! Joy is in the Lord, not in circumstances or hormonal states. Just as Paul rejoiced from prison and Joni Erickson Tada rejoices in physical paralysis, women can rejoice in any condition which will produce joy as a fruit of the Spirit. Joy begins with godly thinking that leads to godly actions. All women can choose to rejoice in Jesus Christ regardless of their circumstances. Self-control of emotions to create a joyful home is a wonderful way a married woman loves her husband and children. Single women can be a calm and steady encouragement and support to their friends and extended family.

Another area in which women require self-control is the area of finances. We mention it here because fiscal wisdom is listed as such a predominant characteristic of the wife to be sought by a wise young man (Proverbs 31:10-31). Maybe this woman is often considered an impossible model because women covet the standards of materialism and beauty that bombard our culture. Rather than strive to emulate the Proverbs 31 woman, they believe they must spend more than is available to attain this unbiblical standard. Married women need to keep their lifestyle and spending under the income of their husbands. Single women need to keep their lifestyle and spending under their own income.

How often men have saved for marriage so that they can truly provide for their wives only to find the woman of interest is steeped in debt. Should he marry her knowing all of his savings for them will be spent to pay for her extravagances? And what might that tell him he has to look forward to after marriage concerning her fiscal responsibilities? Women should equally be on the watch for potential husbands who are irresponsible with money. Biblical counselors will often counsel on self-control in spending.

Next, Paul lists purity as an area for self-control. The presence or absence of this character quality is easily observable in two areas—

conversation and conduct. A married woman protects her husband, her marriage, and other's marriages by her purity. A single woman protects herself, others' marriages, and her Christian brothers by her purity. A pure woman steers clear of inordinate conversations with men. She absolutely doesn't flirt with married men! A pure woman keeps her female body parts covered around any men who are not her husband. With him, it's a totally different story. Then she may become sexually aggressive (1 Corinthians 7:2-5). Female biblical counselors can expect to counsel biblically in this area, and will find excellent coverage of the topic in a book entitled *Intimate Issues* by Linda Dillow and Lorraine Pintus.

Paul attaches the final qualifiers to how a woman keeps her home—with kindness and submission. Notice there is nothing about cleaning one room thoroughly each week! Also, notice there is nothing about dusting and vacuuming methods. Instead, the focus is upon kindness and submission which have to do with the heart of a woman. How often women complain that their husbands don't appreciate all they do for them by cooking, cleaning and dealing with the children. Yet when men allow their hearts to wander when tempted with adulterous thoughts, it is often not to a woman who keeps a nice house but simply to another woman who is kind to them. Kindness and respect are attitudes of the heart that few men can resist (Proverbs 6:24).

Since many women struggle with perfectionism, and not just when it comes to homemaking, kindness is a wonderful replacement for perfectionism! Studies show that perfectionism is a predicting factor for depression.[47] Mothers show kindness in how they respond to the inevitable messes created by children. Wives show kindness in not nagging their husbands about tidiness. Kindness goes hand in hand with submission. A submissive wife is showing kindness when she denies her personal preferences, and keeps her home as her husband prefers. One way single women show kindness is through creating a warm, hospitable home.

---

47 Wei, M., Mallinckrodt, B., Russell, D. & Abraham, W. (2004). Maladaptive perfectionism as a mediator and moderator between adult attachment and depressive mood. *Journal of Counseling Psychology, 51*, pp. 201-212.

Conclusion

Understanding God's perfect design for men and women, Paul the Counselor teaches women to embrace their unique role and purpose for serving Christ. As Christ Jesus submitted to the Father to Whom He was co-equal in His divinity, a married woman submits to her husband to fulfill her God-given role for God's glory alone. Make no mistake about it: others will notice a submissive woman's gentle and quiet spirit and it will bring honor to Christ. In fact, it may bring persecution by those who see your demonstration of humility in willful submission to all authorities, but godly women must not shrink from this awesome opportunity to practically demonstrate God's wisdom in action and to impart these truths to other women through disciple-making and biblical counseling.

PERSONAL CONNECTION QUESTIONS

1. Have you adopted the biblical paradigm of complementarianism as your world view? If not, can you scripturally support an opposite view? Consider conducting a personal research project whereby you journal all the things God says in His Word that refer to your gender. In what ways does this worldview impact your personal relationship with Jesus Christ? With your counsel to women?

2. For women: Name a single woman and a married woman whom you could engage in discussion regarding the importance of biblical womanhood in your lives. You can easily disciple them by reviewing the Scriptures in this chapter with them so that they can decide to join you in showing God's glory on earth and in the universe. Be humble, and confess your own sinful distortions of God's role order. But also, be grateful, and share the victories God's grace empowers.

Chapter 12
A BIBLICAL UNDERSTANDING OF ANXIETY

Howard and Pamela Eyrich

> Rejoice in the Lord always; again I will say, rejoice.
> Let your reasonableness be known to everyone. The
> Lord is at hand; do not be anxious about anything,
> but in everything by prayer and supplication with
> thanksgiving let your requests be made known to
> God. And the peace of God, which surpasses all
> understanding, will guard your hearts and your
> minds in Christ Jesus.
>
> Finally, brothers, whatever is true, whatever is
> honorable, whatever is just, whatever is pure,
> whatever is lovely, whatever is commendable, if
> there is any excellence, if there is anything worthy
> of praise, think about these things. What you have
> learned and received and heard and seen in me—
> practice these things, and the God of peace will be
> with you.
>
> Philippians 4:4-9

How is life going today? Is your child failing in school? Is your car about to die? Are you "under water" with your mortgage? Has your wife separated from you? Is your son getting ready to be deployed? Whatever your situation, you have a lot in common with the Apostle Paul.

In one town, the people were so amazed at Paul's miracles that they were ready to declare him a god and worship him. In another town, the citizens perceived that he was going to be the cause of an economic meltdown so they were ready to stone him. In the midst of a storm, the sailors on board a ship were about to throw him overboard. At a local trial, the Jews were about to get him sentenced to death so he appealed to Caesar and for the next two years carried the uncertainty of that up-coming trial. If anyone could speak to anxiety from personal experience, it would be Paul. If anyone could speak to anxiety from a theological viewpoint, Paul could.

In the New Testament there are three major passages on the subject of worry (worry and anxiety are translated from the same Greek word): Matthew 6:25-33, 1 Peter 5:6-9 and Philippians 4:4-9. In the Matthew passage, Jesus presents a philosophical and yet very simple argument for the foolishness of worrying and the wisdom of trusting God instead. Just prior to his argument as to why we should not worry, Jesus was addressing the issue of our hearts when He said in Matthew 6:21: **For where your treasure is, there will your heart be also.** He then makes a practical application of this truth in Matthew 6:24: **No man can serve two masters; for either he will hate the one and love the other, or he will hold to one and despise the other. You cannot serve God and mammon.** When a Christian attempts to walk the middle of the road, serving both the master of this world (the flesh) and the Holy Spirit of God, there is bound to be anxiety-producing tensions. But Paul moves to the matter of anxiety with this absolute declaration in Matthew 6:25: **Therefore I tell you, do not be anxious for your life. . . .** Why?

What follows is his philosophical yet very simple, logical argument:

Major Premise

Look at the birds of the air. They are utterly dependent upon God. Look at your life. Can you add a single day to your life span? Look at the lilies. They have so little value that they are thrown in the fire and burned and yet God made them with such beauty.

Minor Premise

Your Heavenly father knows that you need all these (earthly) things.

Conclusion

The conclusion is this; God is capable of providing for you. If you will seek first His kingdom and His righteousness; all these things (temporal needs) will be added (provided) to you. Jesus leaves no room for anxiety if we fully trust God.

Peter takes a much more emotional approach, and yet it is also logical. He declares in 1 Peter 5:7: **Casting all your anxiety upon Him, because He cares for you!** Perhaps the picture in Peter's mind when he writes this is his experience of walking on the water. Immediately upon beginning to sink in great anxiety for fear of his life, he cast himself completely upon Jesus. Believing that Jesus cared for him, he cried out, **"Lord, save me!"** (Matthew 14:30). However, if we only pick up on the emotion of the fact that Jesus cares for us, we will miss the foundation for this promise. In 1 Peter 5:6, he exhorts us to **Humble yourselves . . . under the mighty hand of God, that He may exalt you at the proper time.** Humbling ourselves means living in complete dependence upon Him. It is this humility that gives us both the wisdom and the freedom to cast our anxiety upon Him.[48] Peter humbled himself when he cried out, **Lord, save me!**

The third major passage addressing anxiety is written by Paul. In Philippians 4:4-9 above, the Apostle Paul's prescription for dealing with anxiety in Philippians 4 can be characterized as a behavioral approach. It has both emotional and logical components, but overall it is behavioral—*do* this to overcome worry! There are things to do to overcome worry and anxiety in directing your thoughts, words, and actions. You must be intentional and not passive in dealing with worry and anxiety.

The Importance of Knowing God

In conducting our own Family Life Seminars, my wife Pam has three sessions with the wives. She used to begin with the "Role of Wives in Marriage." However, the Lord brought to her mind the fact that there was a prerequisite to fulfilling this role. A woman must begin with an understanding of the character of God. She must not only know God in a personal relationship, she must also *know* God and who He is. As a result, in the first session she now focuses upon knowing God— investigating his character and the implications of his attributes. This provides a woman with a sense of security as she chooses to place herself in submission to her husband.

Knowledge of the character of God also provides a foundation for dealing with anxiety. With Pam's help, then, let's review this fundamental truth as she does for the women in her seminar.

---

48 Space constraints do not allow for the full development of this passage. Suffice it to say that Peter goes on to provide us with practical directions about dealing with Satan and his role in our anxiety as well as reminding us that as Jesus has called us to eternal glory He will in the temporal life perfect, confirm, strengthen and establish us (v 10).

J. I. Packer, in his book *Knowing God*, states: "As it would be cruel to an Amazonian tribesman to fly him to London, put him down without explanation in Trafalgar Square and leave him, as one who knew nothing of English or England, to fend for himself, so we are cruel to ourselves if we try to live in this world without knowing about the God whose world it is and who runs it. The world becomes a strange, mad, painful place and life in it a disappointing and unpleasant business for those who do not know about God. Disregard the study of God, and you sentence yourself to stumble and blunder through life blindfolded, as it were, with no sense of direction and no understanding of what surrounds you."[49]

As believers, we should ask ourselves, to what extent do we know and understand the God that we worship, and what significant difference does it make in our lives? We invest so much time in educating ourselves about the computer, ipad, iphone, social media, sports, movies, politics and a hundred different things that we are particularly interested in at any given time, but how much time is invested in learning and participating in the most significant relationship we will ever have? God desires that we know Him above all else.

Not only does God desire for us to know Him, but knowing Him is a necessity in life: "A right conception of God is basic not only to systematic theology but to practical Christian living as well. This is to worship what the foundation is to the temple; where it is inadequate or out of plumb the whole structure must sooner or later collapse. I believe there is scarcely an error in doctrine or a failure in applying Christian ethics that cannot be traced finally to imperfect and dishonorable thoughts about God."[50] So what are some of the reasons for the study of God?

1. <u>God desires that we know Him,</u> as expressed in Jeremiah 9:23-24: **Thus says the Lord: "Let not the wise man boast in his wisdom, let not the mighty man boast in his might, let not the rich man boast in his riches, but let him who boasts boast in this, he <u>understands and knows me,</u> that I am the Lord who practices steadfast love, justice, and righteousness in the earth. For in these things I delight,"**

---

49 Packer, J.I., *Knowing God,* (London, Holder and Stroughton, 1973), pp. 14-15.
50 Tozer, A.W., *The Knowledge of the Holy*, (San Francisco, Harper & Row,1963), p. 105.

declares the Lord. In Hosea 6:6 we are again reminded: **For I desire steadfast love and not sacrifice, the knowledge of God rather than burnt offerings** (emphasis mine).

2. We realize that God is the source of our being, in Genesis 1:26, where Scripture tells us that we are made in his image, and further on in Psalm 139:13-14, reminds us that He formed our inward parts. Our very life and breath are created and sustained by God. Job was well aware that God was the source of his being, as expressed in Job 10:8-12.

3. God is the author of our history, which begins in Genesis 1:1: **In the beginning God . . . .** The prophet Isaiah in chapter 44:24 reminds Israel: **Thus says the Lord, your Redeemer, who formed you from the womb: "I am the Lord, who made all things, who alone stretched out the Heavens, who spread out the earth by myself."**

4. God is our strength for today and hope for tomorrow. Everything we require to live this life today and to prepare for the life to come can be found in God. Three building blocks so necessary for this life are knowledge (data gathering), understanding (comprehension), and then wisdom as being the appropriate use and application of that knowledge and understanding. Proverbs 2:6-12: **For the Lord gives wisdom; from his mouth come knowledge and understanding . . . .** (Proverbs 2:6-12).

A Portrait of God

Let us go a little deeper and examine more closely a picture of God. Let us quickly clarify that we do not mean the pictures of Jesus superimposed on a collectible dinner plate or a "Jesus clock" and other sundry items that you might find in a Christian bookstore. What we are talking about is the various aspects of His character that, woven together, begin to give us some insight as to how God might appear spiritually. Obviously, this list is not exhaustive but is an attempt to better encourage and excite the believer to pursue the quest of knowing his God and his Redeemer for the purpose of overcoming anxiety and worry.

The first and most important aspect of His character is his holiness. If God in fact is not holy it makes all the other aspects of his character vulnerable. A. W. Tozer stated it well in *Knowledge of the Holy* (p. 105):

> "Holy is the way God is. To be holy He does not conform to a standard. He is that standard. He is absolutely holy with an infinite incomprehensible fullness of purity that is incapable of being other than it is. Because He is holy, His attributes are holy; that is, whatever we think of as belonging to God must be thought of as holy."

Exodus 15:11 emphasizes the holiness of God: **Who is like you, O Lord, among the gods? Who is like you, majestic in holiness, awesome in glorious deeds, doing wonders?**

God's sovereignty is an attribute with which we struggle. When we are in trouble or want a quick solution to a problem we want Him to be in absolute control. However, there are also the times *we* want to be in control and want God to more or less stay out of our business. Whether we are comfortable with this attribute or not, the bottom line is that God is sovereign and sovereignty rules over *all things*. He has complete rule, power and authority over all things and all mankind. He does all things after the counsel of *His own will*. Psalm 103:19 says: **The Lord has established his throne in the Heavens, and his kingdom rules over all.**

His righteousness and his justice in the Scriptures can be seen in "lockstep" with one another. They may be considered two sides of the same coin. Dr. William Evans, a pastor and author in the late 1800's and early 1900's stated:

> "There is a sense in which the attributes of the righteousness and justice of God may be regarded as the actual carrying out of the holy nature of God in the government of the world. So that in the righteousness of God we have His love of holiness, and in the justice of God, His hatred of sin."[51]

---

51 Evans, William, *The Great Doctrines of the Bible,* (Liverpool, England, The Bible Institute Colportage Association, 1912)

God cannot be unfair due to the overriding factor of his holiness.

Splendid and majestic is His work; and His righteousness endures forever . . . . The works of His hands are truth and justice; and His precepts are sure. They are upheld forever and ever; they are performed in truth and uprightness (Psalm 111:3; 7-8).

The three *Omni's* of God are loaded with assurances for the believer. God is Omniscient; He is *all knowing,* according to Psalm 139:1-2. What a comfort to know that He knows our deepest thoughts, frailties, physical needs and spiritual needs. On the other hand, it also means that He knows the sin in our hearts and nothing can be hidden from His eyes. God is Omnipresent; He is *always present everywhere.* In Psalm 139:7-10 we are assured that we cannot escape His presence, this can be both comforting in that it dispels the feeling of aloneness and convicting knowing He sees the sinful choices we make. God is Omnipotent; He is *all powerful.* "The power of God is that ability and strength whereby He can bring to pass whatsoever He pleases, whatsoever His infinite wisdom may direct, and whatsoever the infinite purity of His will may resolve . . ."[52] What an encouragement to the believer who is safely wrapped up in the everlasting arms of our God and our Savior. Therefore, we are not self-confident but *God Confident*!

The immutability of God and the love of God are beautiful compliments to one another. By virtue of the immutability of His character, He never changes (Malachi 3:6). In connection to his immutability, His love never changes in quality or quantity. While we as humans are known to fall out of love as often as we fall in love, depending on the circumstances, God's love is *constant.* We are challenged by Christ's example to demonstrate this kind of love towards others. Just as He loved us and gave His life for us, so also we must love one another (1 John 3:16, 23).

These days we are bombarded with so much information via TV, internet, magazines, radio, blogs, and all forms of social media

---

52 We have been unable to find an original source for this quote. We have found it quoted in several places and attributed to Charnock but without references. We are satisfied that it comes from Charnock and likely from his *Existence and Attributes of God.*

so that we have difficulty in trying to discern what is really true and what is not. Fortunately for us, the <u>veracity of God</u>, meaning that God's Word is truth and is wholly trustworthy, affords us great comfort. In Psalm 119:151, 160, David testifies to the truthfulness of God's Word. **"And all Thy commandments are trust . . . . The sum of Thy word is truth. And every one of Thy righteous ordinances is everlasting."**

What does that mean for us? God is the God of truth. He is possessed of stability, reliability, firmness, and trustworthiness. He is a Person who is entirely self-consistent, sincere, realistic, and undeceived. God cannot lie by virtue of His holiness and righteousness.

Though there are many more attributes of God, for our purposes in addressing anxiety, a final attribute we see is <u>God's eternality</u>. His existence is unending, with no beginning. All of God's attributes have always existed and continue to exist with the same measure of power as before (Psalm 102:24-27).

Practical Implications

What could we consider a practical implication of our study? God is always present in the fullness of His glory and power. He never grows weak or feeble; never suffers from forgetfulness; never is surprised by a sudden turn of events; never fails to keep His promises; never finds His plans thwarted; and never ceases to be true to His spoken Word. When we accept these truths about God and incorporate that thinking into our daily lives, it can't leave much room for anxiety. We, being created in the image of God, are marked for eternity to come. Of course, where and how we spend it is determined by our relationship to His Son, Jesus Christ.

In Isaiah 6:6, the prophet Isaiah caught a glimpse of a holy God and, in so doing, he saw the awfulness of his own sin. A high view of God will give us a proper perspective of ourselves and will teach us to fear His name as well as worship Him. This can serve to be the greatest motivator to service as well as the greatest inhibitor to sin.

Now with this context, note where Paul begins his model of anxiety deflection in Philippians 4:4: **Rejoice in the Lord!** Rejoicing is a form of praising, so let us focus on *praising* the Lord as the first "P" that Paul teaches in this passage. It may surprise you that the most important word in this command is not **"rejoice"** (praise), but **"LORD!"** For example, we can rejoice in recruiting the top player for our football team but it will not allay our anxiety about advancing to the national championship. Our recruit might get hurt. While he is a great asset to the team, the player is not unchallengeable.

Therefore, the most important word in this command is **"LORD!"** Hence, we need to ask the question: "Who is the Lord and what relationship does He have to our anxiety-producing situation?" In essence Pam is teaching the women in her seminar that their trust is ultimately in the Lord and I teach counselees that they must root their behavior in overcoming anxiety in God's character. Ultimately, what Paul is teaching here in Philippians 4 is that trusting the Lord must replace anxiety. So here is the first assignment for the anxious counselee.

I say to my counselee, "Paul is instructing you to praise (rejoice in) the Lord. So, I want you to make a list of at least five of God's character traits. Once you have the list I want you to take each trait and write out in two or three sentences how God in that character trait relates to your situation." With few exceptions these are the five traits people list (though they do not always use the technical words to express the trait): sovereignty, omnipresence, omnipotence, omniscience, immutability and love. For example, with regard to sovereignty the counselee may write:

- "God is in control of all things so I can be assured that God is in control of my surgical procedure."
- "God is omnipresent so I know that God will be in the operating room with me."
- "God is omnipotent so I know he has the power to rule and overrule whatever occurs during the procedure."
- "God is omniscient so I know that God knows every detail of my body and he knows any weakness my surgeon may have and can compensate."
- "God is immutable and therefore I can be confident that He cannot fail."

By developing the truth of these characteristics within our thinking, we cultivate a basis for trust in God that lays the foundation for the following instructions.

The second "P" of Paul's instruction is to *prohibit* your anxiety (v.6). The immediate response of most people is, "Ok, I know that! But that is what I cannot do!" That is a legitimate reaction. We have all perhaps been in the anxious position of trying to pay a bill for which we do not have the immediate funds. Since paying our debts is an imperative, that means it is a command from God and not an option. And, with God's imperatives come God's promises to empower us through the Holy Spirit to carry out the instruction (Acts 2:17; Luke 24:49; Romans 8:9). So, we can choose to stop the worrying by implementing Paul's entire model as we will see in the next portion of the passage.

The third "P" is the command to *pray* (v.6.) Paul gives a specific context for prayer—with thanksgiving. In a counseling session I like to have the counselee draw a line with an arrow on each end. The arrow pointing left reminds the counselee to look backwards and remember another worrisome situation in which God faithfully brought him through. The arrow to the right encourages the counselee to pray in faith, believing and exercising that faith by thanking God that he can be assured that God will meet the current unforeseen event.

The fourth "P" bids the counselee to *possess* the mind (v. 8). Paul gives some very specific directions for accomplishing this task. In counseling, I ask the counselee to take each of the topics that Paul lists and determine three examples of that topic that are particularly meaningful to him or her and write them out on a 3x5 card that can be used to focus upon in carrying out Paul's instructions. A variation of this assignment is to have the counselee list five people with whom they can connect with in a productive activity that engages the mind.

The final "P" in the model laid out here by Paul to deal with anxiety is this: *practice* what I have taught you and what you have seen in me, do (v.9). The ESV translation uses the word "do." The NASB translates it as practice. I prefer the latter. If we review the life of Paul we see him "practicing what he preaches." The word practice conveys the idea of intentional planning. That is what Paul is driving home. Paul indicates that there are two results of this practice:

First, in verse 7 he indicates that the peace of God that surpasses all comprehension (we will not be able to explain the calm that comes over us) will guard our hearts (emotions) and our minds (thinking).[53] The second product is found in verse 9: the God of peace will be with you. Yes, God is always with us because He indwells us by the Spirit. The impact here is that as we practice this model we will have a conscious awareness that the God of peace is with us.

Around our church I am part of a group of men known as the "zipper club." We all have that telltale stitching over our breastbone resulting from bypass surgery. As of this writing, it has been over eight years since I underwent surgery. When you know the doctor is going to invade your chest cavity, stop your heart, and re-plumb the piping inside of you, it is an anxious event. I have a low tolerance for pain, so I am not the best medical procedure candidate. But, the Lord enabled me to practice Paul's prescription and as soon as I could whisper, I told my wife Pam that I have now experienced the fullness of the promise of a peace that passes comprehension. God was faithful!

Paul has outlined for us a model to implement the reasonable argument of Jesus' exhortation in Matthew 6:25, **"Therefore, do not be anxious"** about food, drink, clothing or whatever tomorrow may bring. His model provides us with a mechanism by which we can "cast all our cares on Jesus." Peter encouraged those early Christians who found themselves without food, shelter, and a means to earn a livelihood, giving them complete confidence that God cared for them.

Each of the components of Paul's model can have diverse elements. For example, I saw three different people in my counseling practice recently who were anxious. Each situation was very different. One man was concerned about a coming meeting with a shepherding team of his church board regarding his marital problems. The second was a couple faced with financially assisting family members. The third was an individual anticipating a meeting regarding a difficult employment situation. The components of the model were applicable

---

53 Here is a more literal translation that is a bit awkward: Rejoice in the Lord at all times; again I say rejoice; so that your forbearing spirit (may) be known to all people. The Lord is near (there is) nothing to be anxious for. But in everything the prayer and supplication with thanksgiving the requests of you make known to God and the peace of God that surpasses all understanding will guard your hearts and minds.

but the execution of the implementation had to be tailored to each unique situation.

The biblical counselor as well as the everyday believer can turn to the Apostle Paul for a model to implement the promise of Jesus, the Son of God; "come unto me all ye who labor and are heavy laden and I will give you rest." Anxiety is fraught with restlessness. Rejoicing trust in the God who is the same yesterday, today and forever coupled with thankful prayer and a mind-set that is fixed on Jesus transforms anxiety into peace, and a heart at rest.

PERSONAL CONNECTION QUESTIONS

1. To overcome anxiety, Paul instructs us to begin with praising the Lord and rejoicing in Him. Make a list of at least five of God's character traits in the Bible (hint: Psalms is a rich book to research). Once you have the list, take each trait and write out in two or three sentences how God in that character trait impacts your situation. Common attributes clearly seen in Scripture are God's sovereignty, omnipresence, omnipotence, omniscience, and immutability or love.

2. How would you counsel someone to overcome their anxiety and worry? Write out an agenda with Scriptures you would teach and homework you would assign to them to address this problem specifically.

Chapter 13
PAUL AND PHARMACEUTICALS

Kurt Grady and Phillip Price

**No longer drink only water, but use a little wine for
the sake of your stomach and your frequent ailments.**
2 Timothy 5:23

The discussion of medication use by people of various faiths is
neither brief nor is it simple. As medications have become a staple
in our society, particularly over the past 100 years, questions have
arisen. Some have taken a position that all medications are "wrong."
Others have arrived at the opposite conclusion, welcoming all
medications for any purpose. Many live somewhere in the middle,
but most have really not given the matter serious study against the
backdrop of Scripture. In this chapter, we hope to bring several issues
to light for in-depth consideration. Our scope will be broad and we
will likely generate more questions than we answer. It is our heartfelt
desire, however, to drive our readers back into Scripture, to Godly
discernment and to a place where they can be confident that the
conclusions we have arrived upon are well informed, scientifically
supported and, most importantly, scripturally sound.

Of particular interest to us in the framework of a biblical
counseling model of personal disciple-making is the question
surrounding the legitimate use of medications in the treatment of
what the world would call "mental disorders." This, too, is a complex
subject, yet one which we want to address. Though various chemical
compounds have been used for centuries to treat that which ails man,
the launching point for the modern pharmaceutical era rests in the
1950's with the discovery of a host of medications for a variety of
mental problems. While the modern era begins here, Scripture is
not completely silent on the matter of treating sicknesses with more
than prayer. The use of wine as a medication is well documented in
the ancient world. The Talmud, Hippocrates, Pliny, and Plutarch all
refer to wine as a treatment for various stomach ailments.[54] Because

---

54 Marckwardt AH, Cassidy, FG, McMillan JB (eds/) Webster Comprehensive Dictionary. International Edition. J.G. Ferguson Publishing Company,
1992(1):365.

of its physical and psychological effects we will consider wine as a prototypical medication, since it is one of the few pharmacologically active substances mentioned in the Bible.

Paul to Timothy

1 Timothy 5:22-23 states: **Do not be hasty in the laying on of hands, nor take part in the sins of others; keep yourself pure. No longer drink only water, but use a little wine for the sake of your stomach and your frequent ailments.** It is noted that, in his efforts to maintain purity or asceticism, Timothy drank only water. Perhaps Paul was gently instructing him that purity (5:22) and asceticism were not one in the same? In his time, as it still is today in many parts of the world, water was often contaminated with infectious microorganisms which caused fever, nausea, vomiting, diarrhea, and the like. If this contamination were to continue over time, it could lead to chronic dehydration and malnutrition and thus weakness and generally poor well-being (**"frequent ailments"**). However, it was a common practice to mix wine with water or to drink wine in place of water since the alcohol in the wine would kill bacteria and neutralize viruses that lead to various illnesses. This seems to be what Paul is referring to in his letter, not overlooking his use of the phrase **"a little wine."** Paul knows that Timothy has stomach problems and he knows that he has frequent ailments (that are perhaps related to the former). Paul was suggesting *a little wine* be used as a medication to treat symptoms he had either directly observed or had been reported to him by others. Paul was not condoning drunkenness or a departure from the purity he mentions earlier. To the contrary he was telling his young disciple to use wine, the only medication he had available to him to treat and/ or prevent a real physical condition that likely led to further physical complications.

Other than a concern for his friend, what other aim might Paul have in mind? As one who held a singular focus on his calling, Paul was no doubt also interested in Timothy's effectiveness as an Elder of the Ephesian church. If Timothy were physically weak and sickly, he would be less impactful as a leader. Thus, Paul was not only concerned about his physical well-being, but also his spiritual well-being. If we attempt to apply this teaching to Christians in the present, we can safely say that the use of medications to treat a known physical malady was encouraged with an end goal of being more effective in one's work in the Kingdom.

Paul to the Church at Ephesus

When it comes to the psychoactive effects of wine, Paul has a somewhat different point of view. The intoxicating effects of wine are well known to all of us. Over the years wine has been used medically for its sedating effects and even as a general anesthetic. As a student of the Old Testament, Paul would have been familiar with the prohibition and the prescription that God gave us regarding the use of wine in Proverbs 31:4-7: **It is not for kings, O Lemuel, it is not for kings to drink wine, for rulers to take strong drink, lest they drink and forget what has been decreed and pervert the rights of all the afflicted. Give strong drink to the one who is perishing, and wine to those in bitter distress; let them drink and forget their poverty and remember their misery no more.**

God specifically forbids the ingestion of alcohol for its intoxicating effects while allowing its use as an anesthetic, sedative, and pain killer. This allowance is made for extreme cases much in the same way that we might give Morphine to a dying cancer patient. With this in mind, let's look at a rather odd comparison Paul makes in Ephesians 5:18: **And do not get drunk with wine, for that is debauchery, but be filled with the Spirit.** Why did Paul make this distinction between being intoxicated and being filled with the Holy Spirit? Why did he select that particular sinful behavior to contrast with being Spirit-filled? Could it be that Paul realizes that people will often turn to things in the creation (like medications) rather than the Creator when dealing with spiritual problems? Basing our conclusions on a few verses would be unwise so let's take a look elsewhere in the Scripture to determine if the conclusions we have drawn are valid.

James to the Church

In James 5:14, it states: **Is anyone among you sick? Let him call for the elders of the church, and let them pray over him, anointing him with oil in the name of the Lord.** In writing to the church, James infers that Christians can and do become physically sick. We become sick as the result of sin. Ultimately, all sickness results from Original Sin through which sickness and death entered the world. But often sickness can be traced directly back to personal sin (Exodus 15:26; Leviticus 26:14-16; Deuteronomy 12:7-16; John 5:2-9, 14). We can also directly observe situations where this is the case. For example, those who regularly choose to consume large amounts of alcohol over a long period of time are likely to develop physical consequences. Alcoholic liver disease is directly related to the sin of drunkenness. The same logic could be applied to a variety of other sins and resultant physical sicknesses. Of course, many other diseases are not related in this way.

By the use of his language and choice of words, it is clear James is talking about a weakness in the physical body when he refers to being sick. He is not referring to a spiritual weakness of the flesh. That matter is handled elsewhere. It is also clear that not all people who live Godly, devout lives will be free from illness and, conversely, those Christians who sin repeatedly are not necessarily destined for physical sickness. In short, sickness happens, at some point, to all of us. In the absence of Christ's return, we will all eventually succumb to a death due to illness or injury.

What are James' instructions? If he is so profoundly weak that he cannot get up and go to the church, he calls for the elders. Notice how the emphasis here is on calling the elders and not on calling the physician. A very close review again of the language shows that the elders were to literally rub him down with oil while praying for him. This was not a ceremonial anointing as we think of it today. It was a rubbing down with oil, not for sacred purposes, but for medicinal purposes. Oil, in that time, was considered to be therapeutic, and in the context of James' language and word choices, this is what he intended us to know.

How do we apply James' instructions today? First, let us not neglect the ministry of visiting the sick and praying for the sick. These are both vital responsibilities of the local church. While we no longer utilize oil as medication *per se*, we can conclude that James endorsed the use of medication when appropriate to do so. Perhaps the elders were called in to work with the person who was sick in order to determine if there was a particular sin or pattern of sins that had led to their physical condition. We believe this can apply today as well. While medications are still useful today, when a Christian is suffering the physical consequences of personal sin, it is important to deal with these matters spiritually in addition to treating the physical consequences medically. From Paul's writings, James, and Proverbs, we can make the following conclusions:

1. The use of medications is permissible and even encouraged for treating physical sicknesses.

2. One of the reasons we seek to treat physical sickness is to allow the believer to be more effective for their work in the Kingdom.

3. Sinfulness, if present, should be dealt with spiritually, while physical sickness should be addressed medically.

Identifying the Problem

Most believers would agree with Paul and recognize the benefits of using medications for medical conditions such as diabetes, hypertension, cancer, infections and the like. In the area of biblical counseling, however, we are more often dealing with worry, anxiety, fear, depression, bipolar disorder, and a host of other spiritual-emotional issues. The world would consider these to be medical conditions as well. While we will explore the definition of disease shortly, we must first understand something about our problems in general.

The basis for all things in what we will call the "seen world," lies in the "unseen world." The effects of what is going on in the spiritual realm often manifest themselves in the physical realm. Everything we experience through our five senses is either impacted or caused by something occurring in the "unseen world." To put it another way, our daily lives are largely the fruit of what is happening in the spiritual realm, which means that what is happening spiritually forms the root or basis of what is taking place in our daily lives. We would view the happenings in the Heavenly realm as the "causes" and the downstream results in the physical world as the "effects." Since man's creation and his subsequent Fall (Genesis 3), he has been a target of the evil fallen realm. Note Ephesians 6:12: **For we do not wrestle against flesh and blood, but against the rulers, against the authorities, against the cosmic powers over this present darkness, against the spiritual forces of evil in the Heavenly places.**

There is truly a battle going on. It is an unseen battle where the angelic host is locked in a literal war for purity and holiness against horror and evil. If we are going to be really successful at dealing with the problems in our lives, we are going to have to think differently about how we engage those problems. Applying our human problem solving skills in this world can lead to improvement in those general problems, but the important thing to remember is that the improvement is temporary at best. If the root of our life difficulties is really in the spiritual realm, it is at this level where we must wrestle if our desire is permanent improvement. More specifically, if counselees are wrestling with worry, anxiety, fear, depression, bipolar disorder, or the host of other matters often referred to as "diseases," we must work in the Heavenly places for a permanent solution. Medications *may* address some physical issues, but they do not address the spiritual matters. Medications can provide some people with symptom relief but this is a temporary improvement at best.

Understanding Disease

The following is taken from our book, *Deceptive Diagnosis*:

> This is a vast topic in the context of a single chapter. We have limitations that will only allow us to touch on subject areas that require significant exploration. There is much to consider beginning with the relationship of God to science, our presuppositions, and where our ultimate authority rests. Our aim then, is to simply engage the reader to stimulate probing and provocative questions and to challenge truth in the physical realm against the transcendent Truth of Scripture.[55]

We live in a society where anything from pregnancy to poor childhood behavior is considered by some to be a disease. It seems that the experts are just as confused about the definition of disease as is our culture. According to Webster's Comprehensive dictionary, disease is defined as "disturbed or abnormal structure or physiological action in the living organism as a whole, or in any of its parts." In *The Role of Diagnosis in Psychiatry*, British psychiatrist R.E. Kendell says, "There is no concept in medicine more fundamental than that of disease or illness."[56]

---

55 Tyler, David and Grady, Kurt, *Deceptive Diagnosis: When Sin is Called Sickness,* (Bemidji, MN: Focus Publishing, 2006)

56 Kendell, R.E., *The Role of Diagnosis in Psychiatry*, (Oxford Blackwell Scientific Publications, 1975), p.145.

Conversely, Dr. Thomas Szasz, a secular psychiatrist and well-known critic of psychiatry who has authored hundreds of papers and books, says of disease: "All too often the problem of defining disease is debated as a question of science, medicine, or logic. By doing so, we ignore the fact that definitions are made by persons, that different persons have different interests, and hence that differing definitions of disease may simply reflect the divergent interest and needs of the definers." Szasz goes on to say: ". . . the decisive initial step I take is to define illness as the pathologist defines it—as a structural or functional abnormality of cells, tissues, organs, or bodies. If the phenomena called mental illness manifest themselves as such structural or functional abnormalities, then they are diseases; if they do not, they are not."[57]

Janet Vice, Ph.D. (Philosophy) says: "Any person whose behavior is deviant or socially unacceptable as the result of a brain disorder is suffering from a neurological disease, not a mental illness. Mind is an abstract term whose referent has not yet been clearly defined and whose nature remains speculative. Unlike bodies, which can be seen, touched, and located in space, minds are inferred from bodily and linguistic behaviors."[58] Dr. Vice, like many in our culture, believes that man is basically good, so therefore, any bad thinking or poor behavior that occurs must be caused by some physical abnormality.

Herein lies the conundrum. Is "disease" as it relates to thinking and behavior a real, tangible thing or is it simply an idea or philosophy? Is the term used out of convenience in order to achieve some other goal? The general population does not ask these questions. When they hear the media, or respected researchers from prestigious universities, the government, or other authorities make claims about mental illness being a disease, they assume it is true. When they hear terms like "chemical imbalance" and "neuro-biochemistry," or information about the latest breakthrough medication for bipolar disorder, they are certain to accept the word of these "experts." The "biological basis for mental disease" phenomenon has permeated our culture and has been accepted as truth.

---

57 Szasz, Thomas, *Insanity: The Idea and its Consequences*, (New York, John Wiley and Sons, 1987), p.145.
58 Horwitz, Allan V., *Creating Mental Illness*, (Chicago, The University of Chicago Press, 2002), p.22.

Interestingly, not a single drug used in psychiatric medicine holds a definitive mechanism of action. For example, we know how penicillin binds to and subsequently destroys the cell wall of a bacterium. We know how a beta-adrenergic agonist binds to a beta-receptor in the smooth muscle of the lung and subsequently causes bronchodilatation. However, a quick read through the Physicians Drug Reference shows us that the drugs for mental health conditions are described much less definitively. They are "thought to" elicit a particular action on a specific nerve or cause the reuptake or the secretion of this or that neurotransmitter.

The cold fact is we have *no real idea how these drugs work* in a "normal" human brain, much less one "diseased" with some as yet unidentified physical pathology we conveniently call schizophrenia, narcissistic personality disorder, agoraphobia, attention deficit hyperactivity disorder, bipolar disorder, or the like. Although sometimes these labels can help us categorize and identify specific behavioral symptoms, there is no indication of physical causality. Pragmatically speaking, the drugs do seem to elicit improvement in some people so we say they "work." No one can say, with authority, however, exactly how they do what they do. We do not know why they work in some people and not in others. We do not understand why they stop working and we have no idea what is really going on when we begin to mix these chemicals in the bodies of people with troubled minds.

What does this mean in the context of personal redemptive discipleship? If we believe that our problems are rooted in the spiritual realm, it really does not change a thing. If we believe what the Bible teaches, then our battle is not in this physical realm. All the theories about disease and chemical imbalances are simply fallen man's attempt to describe and understand the physical world around him. Are there truly anatomical and physiological changes (effects) that occur in the brains of those labeled as schizophrenic? What about anxiety disorder, depression, or bipolar disorder? What does science tell us? What does Scripture tell us?

Again, if we believe Scripture, then we can conclude that the drugs are not the final answer for "psychological" problems because they do not address the spiritual needs of the Christian who is struggling. Drugs affect the physical and not the spiritual. Should we tell people the drugs are "wrong" or even sinful?

Why Presuppositions Matter

How we answer the question of the presence or absence of disease, particularly within the context in which we are operating in this chapter, is often based on certain presuppositions we
hold. It seems that our growing appreciation for what we believe science is attempting to explain is, in some way, diminishing the value we place on God's Word. We need to remember that science is simply a tool that man uses in an attempt to describe and explain what he observes in the universe. Science today is different than science was three-hundred years ago. For one thing, the very definition of science has changed.

Men like Newton, Boyle, Kepler, Kelvin, Pasteur, Maury, Faraday, Maxwell, Ray, and Linnaeus laid the groundwork for modern science during the time of the Reformation and the Great Awakening. They believed that science was about discovering facts or knowledge about how God had ordered His universe. Modern science has taken on a philosophy that excludes God (materialism) and places man at the center of his universe (naturalism). As a result, science today has been shifted from discovering facts or knowledge to discovering "truth."

Science is not only in the business of obtaining verifiable information. Because of its materialistic-naturalistic orientation, it is in the business of attempting to explain what the facts mean and how we are to view them. In short, modern science is attempting to shape our worldview to a Godless, man-centered universe. Is science therefore evil? No. Science is still science in the purest sense; it is about discovery. It is when science morphs into a self-defined philosophy that we get into trouble. The reorientation of the interpretation of science from a God-centered universe to a man-centered universe is nothing more than an overarching strategy of the enemy in his spiritual battle for the hearts of man. He is a deceiver and he is hijacking science for his own purposes.

With this in mind, it is imperative that we look at science critically. Who is interpreting the facts and what are their presuppositions? Neither Paul nor James were scientists. They were, however, men who had a personal relationship with Jesus Christ, the very Author of science. They did not need Ph.D.'s in biochemistry to see that sin had to be handled in a prescribed manner and that physical problems should be dealt with in another way. They understood that man's problems are rooted in the spiritual realm. We attack those in like manner, spiritually.

Medications *May* Address the Physical

Medications used to treat various mental health conditions do have effects in some people. How they do what they do is not well explained in the scientific literature, despite what we hear broadcast through the popular media. There is currently a debate in some academic circles as to whether or not prescription drugs are effective in treating depression. There is a growing body of evidence showing that they may be no more effective than a placebo.

Antidepressants seem to be able to lift feelings of gloom and depression, but there are legitimate scientific questions as to whether or not the active ingredients actually provide the relief. A number of studies seem to demonstrate that just the act of taking a pill one believes will make them better can provide relief from depression. In short, are we seeing a true pharmacological effect with these drugs or is it just the placebo effect demonstrating the power of hope?[59]

Various medications are also used for treating anxious feelings and they do help some people to be less anxious. However, there is a "cost" involved. These medications often cause some level of drowsiness, impaired judgment, and depressed coordination. Do they really deal with anxiety, fear and worry, or do they simply numb the senses to the point that the things causing these feelings are simply anesthetized? Moreover, we should exercise great caution in attempting to interpret feelings. The United States Food and Drug Administration (FDA) will not allow a medication to be approved in this country based on how it makes someone feel.

---

59 Vice, Janet, *From Patients to Persons: The Psychiatric Critiques of Thomas Szasz, Peter Sedgwick and R.D. Laing,* (New York, Peter Lang Publishing, 1992), p.15.

In fact, the FDA requires that every drug must be approved for a disease. If we follow this line of thinking, we can see why there are many theoretical explanations and descriptions for our struggles in life. We do believe there are pathological, anatomical, and physiological processes that occur in some people (diseases). However, we also believe much of what troubles man is more related to sin than to sickness. The mental health industry and the pharmaceutical industry have done a remarkable job of convincing the masses of their various and widespread mental illnesses in order to generate appointments and prescriptions. Thus, many of man's problems that are "diagnosed" as mental illness are nothing more than sinful man thinking, behaving, and feeling according to his nature.

Could it be that feelings of anxiety, depression and the like are the warning signs that God has graciously provided in our inner being to tell us that something is not right? When we see a warning light on the dashboard of our car, we do not try to break the light to solve the problem; we address the root cause. When these emotional symptoms occur we need to address the underlying causes which are usually spiritual and not physical. The process of examining our hearts is hard work and not as easy as taking a pill.

In every one of these situations, there is a prominent place for heavy doses of the Gospel and an obedient adherence to what is taught in Scripture. While some may indeed require medications for a legitimate physical abnormality (that no one can definitively describe or prove), medical practitioners are simply guessing at what the right cocktail of medications will be to provide relief. When we do not know what the real abnormality is and we do not know exactly how each of the drugs works in a living human being, the result is trial and error.

Conclusion

We can all be thankful for the common grace God has afforded us through the advancements that have been made in medical science. We do not have to think long before coming up with an example of how our lives or the lives of others have been positively impacted by the appropriate use of medicine. Finding ways to prevent and cure diseases are implicit in God's command to subdue the earth. As in all areas of life we must judge the use of medication through the lens of God's Word. When we examine the Scripture and reflect back to Paul's writings, James, and Proverbs, we understand that the Bible encourages the use of medications for treating physical problems.

At the same time we are reminded that sin and the mental problems it causes must be dealt with spiritually. Even if psychiatric medications do provide some symptomatic relief, we need to ask ourselves, are we interested in treating symptoms alone or in finding a solution to the root of the problem? Most often, psychiatric issues can be effectively treated with a large dose of the Gospel of Jesus Christ and the application of His Word. We must always remember that God has given us everything we need pertaining to life and godliness (2 Peter 1:3).

PERSONAL CONNECTION QUESTIONS

1. What are three biblical teachings from Paul's writings, the book of James, and Proverbs regarding medications as outlined in this chapter?

2. All medications have side effects. With so many new drugs on the market each year, how must a Christ-follower view medicine in general and apply biblical principles to this difficult question?

3. Some problems may require both a physical and spiritual remedy. For the disciple-maker and biblical counselor, the spiritual work can always be addressed first in terms of dealing with root issues and often a physical problem presents an opportunity to share the hope of the Gospel for eternal life. As a minister of the Gospel, what other passages of Scripture can you research to help you to think about physical ailments and suffering biblically for the purpose of leading someone to trust Christ more?

Chapter 14
OUR BLESSED COMFORT
AND FUTURE HOPE

Randall Price and Bill Hines

> For the grace of God has appeared, bringing salvation for all people, training us to renounce ungodliness and worldly passions, and to live self-controlled, upright, and godly lives in the present age, waiting for our blessed hope, the appearing of the glory of our great God and Savior Jesus Christ, who gave himself for us to redeem us from all lawlessness and to purify for himself a people for his own possession who are zealous for good works
> Titus 2:11-14

> For the Lord himself will descend from Heaven with a cry of command, with the voice of an archangel, and with the sound of the trumpet of God. And the dead in Christ will rise first. Then we who are alive, who are left, will be caught up together with them in the clouds to meet the Lord in the air, and so we will always be with the Lord. Therefore encourage one another with these words
> 1 Thessalonians 4:16-18

Introduction

Throughout Church history people have avoided the teaching of the prophecy of the end times because it is too controversial or people don't agree. In our day, end times prophecy has enjoyed a revival of sorts. There are many books and web sites on the subject and some pastors speak on the subject often. Yet one area we have noticed that has not been included in writings and sermons concerning the return of Christ is the area of biblical counseling and pastoral care. If Scripture is profitable for correcting behavior and helping people change into Christlikeness (2 Timothy 3:16-17), prophetic passages must be included. After all if things concerning the return of Christ are said to be "**. . . our blessed hope**" (Titus 2:13) and we are told to **". . . encourage one another with these** (prophetic) **words"** (1 Thessalonians 4:18), then biblical counseling is exactly where these prophecies should be implemented.

Knowing that God has a plan and has always had a plan can and should bring immense hope to the one who asks, "How long O' Lord must I suffer?" People suffer for many reasons and in different ways, but all suffering is the result of living in a fallen world and suffering the effects of sin as it comes to bear on our relationship with God, self, others and nature. Yet God has provided a way for man to escape the penalty of sin and to enjoy healing from the effects of sin. Some of the effects of sin are mitigated in the present (forgiveness of sin and growth in Christlike character) and all of sin's effects will be banished in the age to come. We will, therefore, investigate the place of prophecy in counseling and pastoral care by exploring how God's Word confirms that there is: 1) a Messiah for God's people; 2) a comfort for God's people and 3) a hope and a future for God's people.

A Messiah for God's People

In *The Lion, the Witch, and the Wardrobe*, C.S. Lewis' masterpiece of children's literature, Mr. Tumnus the faun lamented to Lucy about the land of Narnia: "Always winter and never Christmas, think of that!" Narnia, under the thumb of the White Witch, was cold, lifeless, and a land with apparently no hope. Winter in Narnia without Christmas meant bondage without deliverance; fear with no hope of joy. Without the birth of Christ, there would have been no Christmas and despair would have overwhelmed humanity. But because it did happen, some 2,000 years ago, the ice of winter is thawing in the hearts of God's people and the eternal spring of new life has begun to break through. No wonder Paul in 2 Corinthians 9:15 exclaimed, **"Thanks be to God for His indescribable gift!"**

Christmas celebrates Christ's first coming. Why did He come? Jesus came to die that people might live. Why was this necessary? Four reasons stand out: 1) to reveal God to man, 2) to redeem man, 3) to rescue man, and 4) to resurrect man.

1. To Reveal God

> **No one has ever seen God; the only God, who is at the Father's side, he has made him known** (John 1:18).

Man needs to know God, but he needed God to make Himself known since man could not go to Him. God the Son made Him known by coming in the flesh so that man could know Him. When man asks the question, "What is God like?" the answer is, "He is like Jesus." To see Jesus is to see God. As the Scripture says, **He is the image of the invisible God, the firstborn of all creation . . . For in him all the fullness of God was pleased to dwell, and through him to reconcile to himself all things, whether on earth or in Heaven, making peace by the blood of his cross** (Colossians 1:15, 19-20).

The coming of Christ was said to be "God incarnate" or God in the flesh. As God in the flesh, Jesus demonstrated what God is like. Jesus showed that God is compassionate as He wept at the tomb of Lazarus (John 11:35-36). He cares about children because Jesus welcomed and blessed the children (Matthew 18:1-2). God is forgiving, shown as Jesus forgave prostitutes and thieves (Luke 7:40-50; 23:39-43). Jesus' willingness to go to the cross, suffering both physically and emotionally (Luke 27:39-46) illustrated the love of the Son for the Father and the Father and Son for man.

Yes, to see Jesus is to see God, for He is God the Son who came in the flesh to redeem mankind and to communicate a love that is both unconditional and eternal for all who believe (John 1:18; 10:24-30; 14:1).

Does God want to know you? He became like you so that He could know and be known by you.

2. To Redeem Man

> **For our sake he made him to be sin who knew no sin, so that in him we might become the righteousness of God** (2 Corinthians 5:21).

A ransom is the price paid to redeem someone from bondage or captivity (Mark 10:45; Hebrews 2:15; Colossians 1:13). To redeem is to buy something back or to buy something out of a situation such as Hosea buying Gomer out of slavery or God buying man out of bondage to sin. Man needed to be freed (1 Peter 1:19; Revelation 5:9). Since man is in bondage to sin (John 8:34), Jesus had to be subject to the same conditions of sinners even to the point of suffering our death (Hebrews 2:14). He had to exchange His righteousness for our unrighteousness (2 Corinthians 5:21). Jesus came to be a ransom for sinners (Matthew 20:28).

> **But now he has appeared once for all at the end of the ages to do away with sin by the sacrifice of himself (**Hebrews 9:26).

Does God love you? He died because He loves you.

3. To Rescue Men

> **Whoever makes a practice of sinning is of the devil, for the devil has been sinning from the beginning. The reason the Son of God appeared was to destroy the works of the devil** (1 John 3:8).

Man needed victory over the devil (Hebrews 2:15) because Satan is the spiritual father of all men from birth (John 8:44), and blinds them to the truth of God (2 Corinthians 4:4). The whole world lies under his control (1 John 5:19). But Jesus came to destroy his hold (1 John 3:8), and to transfer believers to His own spiritual kingdom (Colossians 1:13). If man rejects Christ as his Lord and Savior he has no choice but to be under the sway of the world (1 John 2:15-17), the flesh (Romans 8:8; 12-15), and the devil (1 John 3:8; 4:4). But there is hope for man to be rescued from death.

> **For He delivered us from the domain of darkness, and transferred us to the kingdom of His beloved Son, in whom we have redemption, the forgiveness of sins** (Colossians 1: 13-14).

Are you struggling with things of the world, the flesh, and the devil? Your victory is in Christ!

4. To Resurrect Men

> **I tell you this, brothers: flesh and blood cannot inherit the kingdom of God, nor does the perishable inherit the imperishable. Behold! I tell you a mystery. We shall not all sleep, but we shall all be changed, in a moment, in the twinkling of an eye, at the last trumpet. For the trumpet will sound, and the dead will be raised imperishable, and we shall be changed. For this perishable body must put on the imperishable, and this mortal body must put on immortality** (1 Corinthians 15:50-53).

Jesus lived a perfect life, died as the perfect sacrifice for sin and was raised to new life having triumphed over death the last enemy (1 Corinthians 15:12-26). It is Christ who gives us hope that not only is this life meaningful but eternal life is a certainty (1 Corinthians 15:50-58; 1 Thessalonians 4:16-18). As He is now, so we one day shall be (1 John 3:2). It was Christ's first coming that made possible such a resurrection, and His second coming that will bring it to completion.

But the resurrection life is not only for the future. Paul tells us that there is a present reality to the death and resurrection of Christ. He writes that just as Christ died to sin so we who believe should consider ourselves dead to sin (Romans 6:3) and alive to God (Romans 6:5). In this life before we go to Heaven, we are given a new capacity to say "No" to sin and "Yes" to God. His death has already begun to do its work by setting us free from the death of sin and making us alive to God (Ephesians 2:1-7). Are we perfect as we will be in Heaven? Of course not. We must continue to seek forgiveness for sins (1 John 1:9) and work at living the Christian life by faith (Philippians 2:12-13). But for the first time our faith allows us the freedom to live as those who are risen from death and alive in Christ. **So you also must consider yourselves dead to sin and alive to God in Christ Jesus** (Romans 6:11).

Do you sense that your life has changed since you placed your faith in Christ? He has made you free to live the life He desires for you. He has freed you from the bonds of sin and death and raised you to new life in Him.

A Comfort for God's People

> **For the Lord himself will descend from Heaven with a cry of command, with the voice of an archangel, and with the sound of the trumpet of God. And the dead in Christ will rise first. Then we who are alive, who are left, will be caught up together with them in the clouds to meet the Lord in the air, and so we will always be with the Lord. <u>Therefore encourage one another with these words</u>** (1 Thessalonians 4:16-18, emphasis mine).

People are comforted by different things. Some gain comfort knowing that the facts of Scripture support the truth of their faith. Some want to know that their suffering will end with the added affirmation that what they have suffered will be used by God to bless them and others.

The Old Testament contains specific prophecies concerning the <u>first coming</u> of Christ. Here are a few passages that will drive home the point. These are only a few of over 100 prophecies.

• Born of a virgin	Isaiah 7:14; Matthew 1:18, 24-25
• The Son of God	Psalm 2:7; Matthew 3:17
• The seed of Abraham	Genesis 22:18; Matthew 1:1; Galatians 3:16
• Tribe of Judah	Genesis 49:10; Luke 3:23, 33
• Family line of Jesse	Isaiah 11:1; Luke 3:23, 32
• House of David	Jeremiah 23:5; Luke 3:23, 31; Acts 13:22-23
• Born at Bethlehem	Micah 5:2; Matthew 2:1
• Preceded by a messenger	Isaiah 40:3; Matthew 3:1-2
• Resurrection	Psalm 16:10; Acts 2:31
• Sold for thirty pieces of silver	Zechariah 11:12; Matthew 26:15
• Wounded and bruised	Isaiah 53:5; Matthew 27:26
• Hands and feet pierced	Psalm 22:16; Luke 23:33
• Crucified with thieves	Isaiah 53:12; Matthew 27:38
• Garments parted and lots cast	Psalm 22:18; John 19:23-24
• His side pierced	Zechariah 12:10; John 19:34

There are many more prophecies of the first coming of Christ and illustrations of what He would do but the above should encourage anyone that God does what He promises. Trusting God is the heart of faith as we are told in Hebrews 11:6: **And without faith it is impossible to please him, for whoever would draw near to God must believe that he exists and that he rewards those who seek him.** These prophecies should encourage the believer that they can trust that the promises of God will be kept.

The way the Old Testament points to the birth, life, ministry, death, resurrection, and deity of Jesus should bring great comfort and encouragement. The God who loves provided a sacrifice for all who would come to Him for redemption. He promised a Messiah and He delivered a Messiah. We can trust His promises whether they concern His coming or His ability to help people in our time of need (Philippians 4:19; Hebrews 4:16).

Just as God told us ahead of time that Christ would come, He has told us ahead of time that Christ would return. It is to His second coming that we now look for comfort.

As we look at prophecy concerning the future, a special word is appropriate. Many people differ concerning the time and circumstances of the return of Christ. Some see these differences as issues to separate them from fellowship with brethren of the differing view. This should not be. Whether one is pre-millennial, post-millennial, amillennial or of some other position, fellowship and Christian love should be based on the person and work of Christ. The writers of this chapter stand steadfast in the pre-millennial, pre-tribulation positions concerning the return of Christ. But that does not diminish our love or respect for brethren with a different view of the details of His return. Allow me to share a wonderful example of men who differed eschatologically.

During a local seminar question and answer session with famed apologist and theologian Cornelius VanTil of Westminster Theological Seminary, a student asked Dr. VanTil how Dr. Walvoord (then President of Dallas Theological Seminary) could be so sold out to a dispensational point of view. The student indicated that he considered Dr. Walvoord somehow deluded and expected that Dr. VanTil would share his concern. But he did not know the character of

Dr. VanTil. Kind to the young student but clear in his conviction, Dr. VanTil let all present know that the young man had it all wrong. He went on to say what a pious, Christ-loving man John Walvoord was. He told of how they would often get together for lunch when each was in the other's home town. They got together not to argue about prophetic positions but to fellowship as brothers in Christ. We suggest that this is the example we should all imitate. One should hold firmly the convictions he believes are the true Scriptural positions, yet remain humble in the areas in which scholars and believers through the ages differ, not because it does not matter, but because we all see through a glass dimly (1 Corinthians 13:12). We must trust that in due time God will teach us all what we need to know as we earnestly seek Him (Philippians 3:14-16; Hebrews 11:6).

What all Bible believing Christians do agree upon is that Christ will return! Note the following:

- Paul reported to the Thessalonians that it is Jesus who delivers us from the wrath to come (1 Thessalonians 1:9-10).

- Paul told Timothy that His appearing will come at the proper time (1 Timothy 6:14-15).

- Paul told those living in Thessalonica that at the return of the Lord He will rapture ("catch up") believers who are alive as well as those already dead to meet Him in the air.

- Words about the "rapture" are written for the comfort of God's people as he tells them to "comfort one another with these words" (1 Thessalonians 4:15-18).

- In Matthew 24 Jesus is asked when the trials and tribulations He had described will take place. An important point is that Jesus says they will see many troubling things before His return, but they should not lose heart for He has told them ahead of time and He is returning!

- In Revelation 1 John is told to write about the past, present and the future: **Write therefore the things that you have seen those that are and those that are to take place after this** (Revelation 1:19).

- The book of Revelation was to encourage suffering Christians as it explains history from the first century until the new

Heaven and the new earth. **Blessed is the one who reads aloud the words of this prophecy, and blessed are those who hear, and who keep what is written in it, for the time is near** (Revelation 1:3).

Add to the above the prophecies of Daniel, Ezekiel and Zechariah and we see that the same Scriptures that accurately prophesied the first coming of Jesus can be trusted concerning the truth of His second coming. Though we will suffer as Christians we have the blessed hope of the coming of our Lord and Savior in glory and we should be ready to greet Him in holiness. Therefore it is incumbent upon us as counselors and disciple makers to teach people how to live. As Paul said:

> **For the grace of God has appeared, bringing salvation for all people, training us to renounce ungodliness and worldly passions, and to live self-controlled, upright, and godly lives in the present age, waiting for our blessed hope, the appearing of the glory of our great God and Savior Jesus Christ, who gave himself for us to redeem us from all lawlessness and to purify for himself a people for his own possession who are zealous for good works** (Titus 2:11-14).

A Hope and a Future for God's People

Hope is not gritting your teeth and desiring that something good might happen. Not according to Scripture. According to Scripture hope is a certainty based in what one knows to be true even if the event has not yet taken place. **Hope is always a confident, sure expectation of divine saving actions.** Therefore, hope is a patient, disciplined, confident waiting for and expectation of the Lord as our Savior. That is why in his letter to Titus, which begins with an instruction to teach sound doctrine and continues with an admonition to avoid evil while seeking Christian character, Paul tells us to do these things while waiting for our blessed hope—the appearing of our great God and Savior Jesus Christ (Titus 2:1, 11-14). Paul is saying that the appearing of Christ is a wonderful certainty—**the blessed hope.** If we believe anything in the Word of God we must believe in the return of Christ. Why is His coming referred to as a **blessed** hope? Because it is a blessing that is sure to take place. Blessing here has the sense of bliss, happiness, delight and glory. It should be of great happiness to wait for the return of Christ. The blessing is directly related to the way we live because if we truly know Christ for whom we wait, we will want to wait for Him and no one or nothing else.

Counselors should take special note of Titus 2:12 . . . **training us to renounce ungodliness and worldly passions, and to live self-controlled, upright, and godly lives in the present age.** Training is special to biblical counselors. It reminds us of 2 Timothy 3:16-17 and the Word that teaches us and corrects us, the very thing a coach or trainer would do. It should also remind us of Ephesians 4:20-24 where we are told to put off the old self, be renewed in our minds and to put on the new self, becoming like God in righteousness and holiness. This affirms hope in the Christian. As we walk with Him we become like Him. As we become like Him we trust our God and Father for whatever comes into our lives, knowing that He is at work and He will return and all suffering will end. What is more pertinent to the suffering of people but to know that there is a divine purpose for life, and there is a divine conclusion to life on earth and life beyond this earthly life.

Conclusion

These things of which the writers of Scripture have written are sound doctrine, compassionate admonition and not to be ignored. Why then do we so often fail to see in the pulpits across our land the preaching and teaching of these things? If we want to teach the truth rightly and care for God's people we must include the truth of prophecy concerning the Messiah people seek, the comfort people seek and the future hope that people seek. We must let the people know that while we struggle in this life our Lord of all hope says, **"Yes, I am coming quickly. Amen. Come Lord Jesus"** (Revelation 22:20).

PERSONAL CONNECTION
Hope & the Second Coming of Christ
A Study Guide

The Christian basis for hope is the finished work of Christ on the cross. Everything hinges on that. As we look toward glory we understand that there is yet to come a grand exhibition of the faithfulness of God. That event is known as the second coming of Christ, when He will return to earth bodily gathering His people to Himself and judging the wicked. Christians should take great comfort in knowing that His second coming is every bit as certain as was the first. It is our blessed hope (Titus 2:13).

1. What does Luke 17:26-30; 18:8 have to say about the condition of the world until the second coming of Christ?

2. What do the following verses have to teach us about the fact of the second coming?
   - 1 Thessalonians 1:10; 2:19; 3:13; 4:14, 16-17.

3. According to the following what do we know about the time of Christ's return?
   - Matthew 24:36; 25:13
   - Mark 13:32-33
   - Luke 12:35-40

4. Why do you think we are not told the exact time of Christ's return?

5. How are believer's to behave until the second coming?
   - 2 Peter 3:10-14
   - Luke 12:35-40
   - Titus 2:11-14

6. If you believe that Jesus will return for His own one day, how does or should that change the way you live, think and feel?
   - Live . . . .
   - Think . . . .
   - Feel . . . .

"And behold, I am coming quickly. Blessed is he who heeds the words of the prophecy of this book." **He who testifies to these things says, "Yes, I am coming quickly." Amen. Come, Lord Jesus.**
Revelation 22:7, 20

Chapter 15
PAUL'S MISSIONAL CALL FOR CROSS-CULTURAL COUNSELING

Steve Standridge and Mark Shaw

For "everyone who calls on the name of the Lord will be saved." How then will they call on him in whom they have not believed? And how are they to believe in him of whom they have never heard? And how are they to hear without someone preaching? And how are they to preach unless they are sent? As it is written, "How beautiful are the feet of those who preach the good news!"

Romans 10:13-15, ESV

There are seven billion people in the world. Many of them do not have access to a Bible, a Bible-teaching church, or even a Christian. A missionary friend in Japan reported that there is less than half of one percent of Japanese who claim to be Christians and that there are 600 suicides per week just in Tokyo alone. There is spiritual darkness all around the globe.

If we truly believe what Paul taught in the Scriptures referenced above, then we must be more concerned about what our *feet* look like than what our houses, cars, boats, yards, gardens, and other comfort items look like. In other words, we need to be in the business of raising up disciple-makers who will carry the message globally to a lost and dying world destined for hell unless they hear and believe the Gospel.

The Apostle Paul provides a glowing example of missionary work as one of the greatest missionaries ever used by God. Paul was clearly called by God and set apart by God. By the planned purpose of God, he endured suffering and hardship so that Paul would depend upon God only.

Paul's insights help all believers to increase in boldness and faith in Christ to conquer a world dominated by sin, corruption, evil, suffering, and death. Christians are on the winning team and must lay aside comfort for the crown of life: **¹¹For the sun rises with its scorching heat and withers the grass; its flower falls, and its beauty perishes. So also will the rich man fade away in the midst of his pursuits. ¹²Blessed is the man who remains steadfast under trial, for when he has stood the test he will receive the <u>crown of life</u>, which God has promised to those who love him** (James 1:11-12, emphasis ours). In America, compared to third world countries, we are the **rich man** mentioned in verse 11 above.

This observation was made: "Everyone wants to get to heaven but no one wants to die to get there." Maybe the same idea applies to missions: "Every Christian wants to see the lost saved but few want to sacrifice personally to make it a reality." If the Apostle Paul had chosen comfort over the crown of life, many would not have learned of Jesus and His sacrificial gift of eternal life. Thank God that Paul was not complacent.

One "Glocal" Mission

One of the terms that The Christian and Missionary Alliance denomination (C&MA) coined is *"glocal."* Obviously, *glocal* is not a real word but a combination of two words: global and local. The idea behind *glocal* is simple: prioritize your hometown, then the surrounding areas, and then the world. Acts 1:8 gives us the blueprint for disciple-making and cross-cultural counseling in a missional context: **"…But you will receive power when the Holy Spirit has come upon you, and you will be my witnesses in Jerusalem and in all Judea and Samaria, and to the end of the earth."** The church of Jesus Christ started with the power of the Holy Spirit and spread the good news of the Gospel in their hometown first (Jerusalem), the surrounding areas second (Judea and Samaria), and to the end of the earth third. The narrative of the book of Acts deals with each region in that order. Further study of Paul's missionary experiences would greatly benefit your spiritual walk.

1. Acts 1-7 details the ministry in Jerusalem.
2. Acts 8-12 details the ministry in all Judea and Samaria.
3. Acts 13-28 details the ministry to the end of the earth.

The church started in its hometown. I don't think you can claim to love people on the other side of the globe when you don't love your next door neighbors, co-workers, and other "near ones."[60] Loving your neighbors will naturally extend to loving those in surrounding areas and around the world.

At Vision of Hope where I (Mark) am privileged to serve hurting young women in the context of the local church, we emphasize loving those women God sends to our program, reaching out to serve the surrounding community, and seeking partnerships with ministries and missionaries around the world in that order.[61] Again, it starts with how we do ministry on a daily basis with the persons God sends us and, as we are good stewards of those souls, we pray God will increase our sphere of influence to impact our community and the world. We are concerned about cultivating disciple-makers in our disciple-making process meaning we want people to not be satisfied simply with being a disciple but with becoming a maker of more disciples!

One Global Message

Paul's message in ministry was singular. He preached the Gospel both publically and privately: **. . . how I did not shrink from declaring to you anything that was profitable, and teaching you in public and from house to house (Acts 20:20).** Paul's message was the same in both contexts. Likewise, the biblical counselor's source of truth is the same as the preacher in the pulpit: the Word of God. The biblical counselor relies upon the Holy Spirit to transform the counselee's heart just as the preacher relies upon the Spirit to change the listener's heart.

The message must present both the truth and grace. Jesus in John 1:14 perfectly balanced both: **And the Word became flesh and dwelt among us, and we have seen his glory, glory as of the only Son from the Father, full of grace and truth.** Jesus confronted

---

60 Neighbor means "near one" and applies to anyone that God has sent across your path.

61 Vision of Hope is a 501c-3 non-profit ministry in Lafayette, IN. Go to www. faithlafayette.org/voh for more information about becoming an intern, staff person, or resident.

a rich young ruler in Mark 10:21-22 and the young man's response would appear to be the "wrong" response:

And Jesus, looking at him, loved him, and said to him, "You lack one thing: go, sell all that you have and give to the poor, and you will have treasure in heaven; and come, follow me." ²² Disheartened by the saying, he went away sorrowful, for he had great possessions.

As we learned early this book, the counsel that Jesus and Paul offered people was often in the form of an admonishment designed to bring <u>change that pleases God</u>. That message and type of counsel might not result in warm fuzzy feelings because it challenges the idols of the heart. One thing is certain in this passage in Mark 10: Jesus loved him and perfectly balanced truth and grace in His counsel to the rich young ruler. The reception of that message was sorrow and feelings of wanting to quit (that's what **disheartened** means) and the Bible reveals the ruler's motives in verse 22: he had great possessions he was not willing to give up.

The missionary's message of the Gospel may likewise be rejected for many reasons but that must not be the primary concern of the missionary. The primary concern is being faithful to God by delivering His message. Paul ministered to the wealthy and the poor; to the Greek and to the Jew; to men and women alike. Paul never changed his message to fit his audience but ministered publically and privately presenting the same Gospel message of love for the unloved and hope for the hopeless.

The life of a missionary is challenging in many ways. A pastor once encouraged his congregation to pray for missionaries in this way:

Monday:	Pray that God will meet the needs of their loneliness. (2 Timothy 4:16-17)
Tuesday:	Pray that they will love the people of their ministry. (Galatians 4:19)
Wednesday:	Pray for their health and safety.

Thursday:	Pray for fluency in language and communication skills. Enable them to preach the message of Isaiah 45:22 and John 14:6.
Friday:	Pray for protection against laziness and complacency (Ephesians 4:14). Let them see fruit for their labors as encouragement.
Saturday:	Pray that God will keep them from discouragement. (2 Chronicles 16:9 and 1 Chronicles 20:15b)
Sunday:	Pray that God will minister to their spiritual growth. (Psalm 1:2-3)

One Universal Method

The book of Acts documents the Apostle Paul's missionary journeys and extensive travel using the universal method of disciple-making. He planted churches by planting men—men that he had personally poured his life into over a season of time. It was not Paul saying, "Ok, listen to me preach, take good notes, and then listen again to the next sermon." No, Paul experienced the ups and downs of life as a minister seeking to reach the lost alongside men like Titus, Timothy, and Silas, just to name a few. Paul followed the discipleship model of Jesus who poured Himself into three key leaders among the twelve disciples.

Much emphasis is given to Jesus' sermons (which only a few are recorded in Scripture) yet He interacted daily in a variety of personal ministry moments with His disciples—the woman at the well, Martha, Lazarus, Zaccheus, a blind beggar, a centurion, and many others. These interactions reflect what biblical counseling is all about: relational connection with admonition and / or encouragement when necessary and with an eye on changing for God's glory. The personal ministry of biblical counseling is an excellent approach to reaching the lost in global missions. Biblical counseling is simply a subset in the method of disciple-making.

As the world declines in its physical, political, economic, and spiritual conditions, Christians must seize this opportunity to reach hurting and hardened souls worldwide. Crisis counseling situations are opportunities to point people to Christ in the hope that their faith would be strengthened. Think about it in this way: someone who is struggling may be more open to a new idea for a solution (Christ) than at any other moment in life. That is an opportunity for the missionary!

Cross-cultural counseling for missionaries trained and skilled in biblical counseling as a ministry of the Word is an essential element of disciple-making. As I look back at my years in ministry, I (Steve) value greatly the precious men and women that God has used to mentor and counsel me. Many missionary assignments are especially hard to endure. Some missionary fields have been defined as missionary graveyards due to the high statistics of missionaries never returning after their first term. Pressures can be great. Cultural differences can be overwhelming. Spiritual results can be extremely few and hard to see. But one principle will sustain each and every messenger of the Gospel. This principle is the love of God for each and every individual soul, starting with the missionary himself.

One Love Compels Us

Why is this principle of God's love so powerful? Identification with Christ is the first part of the answer. Being called to serve as global missionaries, disciple-makers, and counselors is to identify with Christ and His mission. Christ was sent to fulfill the Father's plan. The plan was to demonstrate God's love for the world, all men, everywhere.

> **Paul, a bondservant of Jesus Christ, called *to be* an apostle, separated to the gospel of God which He promised before through His prophets in the Holy Scriptures, concerning His Son Jesus Christ our Lord, who was born of the seed of David according to the flesh, *and* declared *to be* the Son of God with power according to the Spirit of holiness, by the resurrection from the dead. Through Him we have received grace and apostleship for obedience to the faith among all nations for His name, among whom you also are the called of Jesus Christ** (Romans 1:1-6, NKJV).

Three important points must be made:

1. It all starts with God's individual call.

Paul had no doubt his mission was a global one. "All nations" is a worldwide program. Just like the Romans, you and I are reading these verses because someone brought the Gospel to our country, and to us. Someone brought the Good News to us by informing us that we were lost and that God was involved in the act of finding us!

You and I have received grace for obedience to the faith! It is not an option. Grace has come to you and me so that we would be *set apart* to be *sent apart*. The Gospel is by its very nature a message and a message exists with the purpose of causing action and movement. It requires individuals who will take it from point A to point B. Simple, isn't it? The word *apostle* means "one sent on a mission,"[62] or *sent one*. Modern day apostles are missionaries, or sent ones. In what proportions are we involved in taking the Gospel message to every corner of the world, especially in the context of biblical counseling? Counseling is not *only* for the United States of America; it is **"faith among all nations!"** One way to preach the Gospel to all nations is through biblical counseling under the authority of a local church. Paul tells us to move beyond the borders of our nation, as there are truly hurting souls everywhere. We can only move in that way when compelled by God's love.

2. Cross-cultural counseling is to be done in humility.

Missionary work can be very lonely for a variety of reasons. But God is faithful to utilize that loneliness for good. God never wastes any type of pain or suffering in the lives of His children. Quite often, God uses loneliness to produce new heart attitudes in us developed through long and lone hours when we only have God to pray to and communicate with. Humility is cultivated in the realization that all our earthly degrees are nothing but dung compared to knowing Christ and the communion of His solitude and suffering on the cross.

The humility that powerfully transpires from Paul's words in Romans 1:11-12: **"For I long to see you, that I may impart to**

---

62 Merriam-Webster, I. 1996, c1993. *Merriam-Webster's Collegiate Dictionary.* Includes index. (10th ed.). Merriam-Webster: Springfield, Mass., U.S.A.

you some spiritual gift, so that you may be established; that is, that I may be encouraged together with you by the mutual faith both of you and me" (NKJV). Paul's words are so full of love and compassion: a longing type of love that was nourished in the furnace of suffering. The suffering of solitude is one way God demonstrates His love, and only a person who has truly experienced loneliness can love and respond to others in this way. There is a deep, heartfelt desire to be united to others who can receive the loving message that comes as a spiritual gift. It is not a cold set of notes translated more or less carefully in another language. Instead, it is a message prepared in prayer through the multiple attempts the apostle Paul made to reach the Romans he had heard so much about. Paul says in verse thirteen: **"Now I do not want you to be unaware, brethren, that I often planned to come to you (but was hindered until now), that I might have some fruit among you also, just as among the other Gentiles."** It is a message bathed in the deep longing and prayer to finally accomplish something that has been greatly desired.

This is not the message coming from a messenger who is motivated by a desire to travel to new countries. It is not about personal gratification, and suffering teaches this lesson well. If humility is not experienced, then personal interest will only come across to others as an act of superiority: the action of a messenger who feels above the indigenous people group that is being reached. That is why humility is so important; it is learned only through experience.

Do you sense any thought of superiority in Paul's words? He says in verse 12: **"that is, that I may be encouraged together with you by the mutual faith both of you and me."** Humility is written all over this phrase. Being a messenger and a counselor in missions is not an act of superiority. It is a humble request to a great God. Romans 1:9-10 states: **"For God is my witness, whom I serve with my spirit in the gospel of His Son, that without ceasing I make mention of you always in my prayers, making request if, by some means, now at last I may find a way in the will of God to come to you"** (NKJV).

3.   **God wants us to be involved in reaching and counseling souls, one at a time.**

Romans 1:16-17 compels us to serve God by lovingly serving lost souls: **"For I am not ashamed of the gospel of Christ, for it is the**

power of God to salvation for everyone who believes, for the Jew first and also for the Greek. For in it the righteousness of God is revealed from faith to faith; as it is written, 'The just shall live by faith' (NKJV).

". . . the righteousness of God is revealed from faith to faith . . . ." Isn't it beautiful? This is what God is simply asking us to do in one simple method of life-on-life disciple-making: He wants us to be involved in reaching souls, one at a time, by sharing our faith to build another's faith in Christ.

The school of suffering and solitude allows the counselor to approach any person, whatever his or her condition, race, or social status. It is about being stripped of all elements that might interfere with understanding the incalculable value of one soul. It is about having God implant deep within our soul the awareness of the great privilege of breathing life into someone who is yet unreached: a new neighbor to be found across the border, who needs us to move to the other side of the ocean. Yes, the Apostle Paul would confirm this and, in his case, it involved even spending countless hours in a variety of perils while getting there:

> **"Three times I was beaten with rods; once I was stoned; three times I was shipwrecked; a night and a day I have been in the deep; *in* journeys often, *in* perils of waters, *in* perils of robbers, *in* perils of *my own* countrymen, *in* perils of the Gentiles, *in* perils in the city, *in* perils in the wilderness, *in* perils in the sea, *in* perils among false brethren; in weariness and toil, in sleeplessness often, in hunger and thirst, in fastings often, in cold and nakedness"** (2 Corinthians 11:25-27, NKJV).

Paul shared in the sufferings of Christ and it made him a better counselor and minister of Gospel-producing love, humility, and perseverance. God has given all of Himself through His sacrificial love and the work of His Son for the salvation and transformation of souls.

God made no distinction of gender, status, or race. God loves them all; and His message of grace and forgiveness received through repentance of sin by faith in Jesus Christ transcends all cultures to all people groups. He paid the highest possible price to enter into a one on one relationship with each of His children. This is a global concept. It overcomes all barriers, all borders, all cultural differences, and all man-made religious systems.

God has reached you and me individually. Each believer has a unique and personal experience of a one on one encounter with Jesus Christ. The Jew, the Greek, you and I – we are all individually valuable and uniquely called by God for a work that no other is called to do but us! It is faith passed on from **"faith to faith."** It is through our personal reading of God's Holy Word that you and I are transformed. It is through personal encounters with God in that Word and by His Spirit that you and I are given specific assignments. It is through lovingly crafted times of suffering and solitude that you and I are prepared to love life—God's life—the eternal life of each and every soul we come in contact with. It is through the fellowship of the church that we spiritually grow in grace. Let us never forget how God has used individual men and women of God connected to the local church family to accomplish amazing tasks. Let us never forget that the work of salvation is not ours but God's.

Do you agree with the statement that there is nothing of greater value than one soul? Jesus said, in Mark 8:36 and 37: **"For what will it profit a man if he gains the whole world, and loses his own soul? Or what will a man give in exchange for his soul?"** Then, in verse 38 Jesus adds: **"For whoever is ashamed of Me and My words in this adulterous and sinful generation, of him the Son of Man also will be ashamed when He comes in the glory of His Father with the holy angels."** One soul reached and saved by the grace of God is worth more than all the riches contained and combined on this earth. Let us remember this every time we are discouraged from living out the priceless privilege of identifying Christ as our Savior and Lord. Paul the Counselor, in our passage of Romans 1, responds with a loud and clear: **"I am not ashamed of the Gospel!"** Is there any reason to be ashamed of a God that has saved us and His Gospel message that has opened our eyes to value eternal life?

The Gospel is the power of God! This is the power and daily fuel of cross-cultural counseling as Mary A. Thompson (1837-1923) penned in an ancient hymn:

> Behold how many thousands still are lying
> Bound in the darksome prison house of sin,
> With none to tell them of the Savior's dying,
> Or of the life He died for them to win.

> *Publish glad tidings, tidings of peace;*
> *Tidings of Jesus, redemption and release.*

> Proclaim to every people, tongue, and nation
> That God, in Whom they live and move, is love;
> Tell how He stooped to save His lost creation,
> And died on earth that we might live above.

> *Publish glad tidings, tidings of peace;*
> *Tidings of Jesus, redemption and release.*

Conclusion

I encourage you to always keep in mind that God is the one who called you and the one who sustains you through all of life's challenges. Please make sure you cultivate a genuine love for the lost and not for your personal agenda. God has one "glocal" mission, one global message, one universal method of disciple-making, and one love that compels us to reach the lost with compassionate counsel. Know your identity is in Christ and ask for God's help in approaching every soul with the humility of one who has been eagerly praying for the privilege of being sent to be used and, yes, to even learn from this person's life.

Success is found in proclaiming the Gospel message and it may be simply in the context of one-on-one disciple-making called biblical counseling. Success is found in faithfully reaching each soul God has prepared with God's message. Let us never forget the responsibility of making disciples by living life with them so that they can see God's love and increase their love, not for us, but for the one Counselor who will never leave or disappoint them. Praise God for giving you the perfect Counselor: the One who is always there, even in the darkest hour.

PERSONAL CONNECTION QUESTIONS

1. How can you serve a missionary in your local church today? How can you pray for a missionary?

2. How can you pray about becoming a missionary and using your God-given abilities in a foreign land to reach souls one at a time?

3. Write and describe times in your Christian journey when you suffered or felt alone. What lessons did God teach you during that time that drew you closer to Him? How does God's plan for periods of time of prescribed suffering drive you to be more humble and more compassionate to others, especially lost souls?

CONCLUSION

Bill Hines and Mark Shaw

**I myself am satisfied about you, my brothers, that
you yourselves are full of goodness, filled with all
knowledge and able to instruct one another.**
Romans 15:14

Paul the Counselor was an amazing man: writer, preacher, leader,
and disciple-maker. His ministry consisted of public preaching,
small group ministry, and personal disciple-making (which includes
the subset of "biblical counseling"). When he counseled, he also
depended upon the Word of God as his source of truth and not the
ideas or traditions of mankind. Also when he counseled, Paul relied
upon the Holy Spirit to guide him as well as to work in the hearts of
those he was privileged to serve. Paul expected to see positive results
in his ministry; likewise, biblical counselors today should expect to
see results in the lives of those they disciple when they utilize the
sufficient Word of Christ, while depending only upon the Holy Spirit
to bring transformational change.

In this book, you have read how Paul admonished and
warned his counselees to make disciples of them. Paul wanted them
to reflect the character of Christ, and his counsel produced conviction
through loving confrontation of sinfulness in their lives, recognizing
the need for change and the power of the Holy Spirit to forgive and
bring lasting transformation. Paul's message was simply the Gospel,
because it is good news to hurting and hardened souls separated
from their Creator.

Temptations for believers are very real and Paul was not an
amateur at addressing them and proclaiming the freedom found in
Christ, as we grow spiritually into the "new man" (Ephesians 4:22-
24). The process of putting-off sinful thoughts, words, and actions and
replacing them with biblical thoughts, words, and actions was a key,
practical tool that Paul taught to those he counseled. This principle
and many others in Paul's writings remain vital in the process of
progressive sanctification and renewing the mind.

Paul blessed those he counseled, offering them God's grace, peace, comfort, and real hope. Paul was not afraid to address anxiety, pharmaceutical concerns, women's issues, race relations, and other topics that seem so controversial in our politically-correct society today! Paul knew that believers had access to the limitless power of the Holy Spirit to enable them to walk in newness of life and to press on despite their troubled past or present trials. The power of Christ was very real to Paul as it should be to biblical counselors today who have an opportunity to share in the Lord's work and to watch the Master Potter shape the clay lives of counselees using His sufficient Word. God is still in the business of transforming lives and turning Jacobs into Israels and Sauls into Pauls.

One of the primary factors that made Paul a competent counselor was not his past sins and failures, but that he was a changed man, **full of goodness, filled with all knowledge and able to instruct one another** (Romans 15:14). Paul left his past behind him and so must any biblical counselor today. Paul's confidence to counsel and in fellow believers to counsel came from His confidence in the power of Christ to fill brothers and sisters with goodness and knowledge. As we study the Word of God and hide the Word in our hearts (Psalm 119:11), the Holy Spirit illuminates that Word, bringing greater understanding of what and how to change for the glory of Christ. Then, the Holy Spirit provides the power to change, as found in Philippians 2:12-13: **Therefore, my beloved, as you have always obeyed, so now, not only as in my presence but much more in my absence, work out your own salvation with fear and trembling, for it is God who works in you, both to will and to work for his good pleasure.** Paul wrote this passage knowing that all glory is given to God for His work to change the will of a person and to provide the power to execute those changes.

God's final product is commonly called the fruit of the Spirit in Galatians 5:22-24: **But the fruit of the Spirit is love, joy, peace, patience, kindness, goodness, faithfulness, gentleness, self-control; against such things there is no law. And those who belong to Christ Jesus have crucified the flesh with its passions and desires.** Even the final results are evidence of the work of the Holy Spirit by God's grace in a person's life for His glory alone.

Paul wrote to the Roman believers that he was confident in the Holy Spirit within them, that they could competently and lovingly **instruct one another**, and the same is true of all Christians today. The word "instruct" is also translated "admonish" in other versions of the Bible. This takes us back to our definition of biblical counseling being a process of warning, stimulating, and encouraging people to Christ-likeness. Paul wanted people to change, and to help them do this he warned them of the dangers of continuing under the sway of the world, the flesh, and the devil. Paul also stimulated them to deal with their sin in a way that brought real victory, and he encouraged them that through the power of the cross, they truly can grow into Christ-likeness.

Notice what Paul writes in Romans 15:14: **"I myself am satisfied about you, my brothers, that you yourselves are full of goodness, filled with all knowledge and able to instruct one another."** He points out that all maturing Christians are called some of the time to counsel others in this manner but it may not be formally in an office of a local church's building. Instead, it could be over coffee or over the back yard fence with one's neighbor. It is in this way that parents are called to instruct and counsel their children and spouses are called to instruct one another in the Word with all wisdom, humility, and compassion. You may be more like the Apostle Paul than you realize, and God may use you just as He utilized him!

It is our hope that the truth proclaimed in this book will challenge you to grow in wisdom and the knowledge of the truth, found in God's Word, while resting in the grace of our Lord and the power of the Holy Spirit, to the glory of God and the good of His people. May His richest blessings be yours in Christ Jesus our Lord.

Contributing Authors

Fred Bucci holds a B.A. in biblical counseling through Master's Divinity School. He is also certified through ACBC, IABC and TAC. He and his wife Lauri serve as full-time biblical counselors in Cleveland, Ohio.

Dr. Ed Bulkley, Ph.D. has been involved in the biblical counseling movement for many years and is the author of the book, *Why Christians Can't Trust Psychology*, a text used around the world in churches, seminaries, universities, and counseling centers. He is President of the International Association of Biblical Counselors (IABC). Dr. Bulkley is the founding pastor of LIFE Fellowship, a Bible church in Westminster, Colorado, where he serves with his wife Marlowe.

Shirley Crowder was born in Nigeria, West Africa, to Southern Baptist missionary parents. Through the years, she has held a variety of positions within businesses, ministries and churches. She is a never-married single woman who is a biblical counselor, certified by The Addiction Connection, a Southern Baptist Disaster Relief Chaplain, and she serves as a pianist and women's Sunday school and Bible study leader at Valley View Baptist Church in Leeds, Alabama.

Dr. Howard A. Eyrich, M.A., Th.M., D.Min. is the Pastor of Counseling Ministries at Briarwood Presbyterian Church, Birmingham, Alabama
President Emeritus and Professor Birmingham Theological Seminary
FELLOW: Association of Certified Biblical Counselors
Certified Credentialed Member of the Academy
American Association of Biblical Counselors

Pamela Eyrich holds a B.A. in Office Administration and has managed two counseling offices established by her husband Howard. Over the past fifty years she has labored in ministry with her husband in youth, pastoral and counseling ministries. She continues to join him in presenting family life conferences. She is the mother of two children and a grandmother of eight.

Dr. Bob Froese holds a Ph.D. in biblical counseling from Trinity Theological Seminary. For nearly two decades Bob has been senior pastor of Faith Fellowship Church in Clarence, NY, where he directs the Faith Fellowship Biblical Counseling Center. It is his great joy to serve the Lord there with his wife Ruth and their four sons.

Ruth Froese writes as one being changed by God through the counsel of Paul the Counselor. Her marriage to Bob, all thirty-five years of it, shines thanks to those glorious principles, which are also her lifeline in the great joy of being a mom to four sons and two daughters-in-law, and to Oma, one sweet granddaughter. Ruth holds a masters degree in biblical counseling and oversees women's counseling at the Faith Fellowship Biblical Counseling Center in Clarence, NY.

Dr. Kurt P. Grady, Pharm.D., M.B.A., D.B.S., serves as an instructor at Gateway Biblical Counseling and Training Center in Fairview Heights, IL; a faculty and board member at Master's International School of Divinity in Evansville, IN; an adjunct faculty member at Calvary Bible College and Seminary in Kansas City, MO; an associate teacher and board member at Overseas Instruction in Counseling in Louisville, KY; and the vice-president of the American Academy of Biblical Counselors. He has co-authored two books: *Deceptive Diagnosis: When Sin is Called Sickness* and *ADHD: A Deceptive Diagnosis*. Kurt works in the neuroscience biotechnology/pharmaceutical sector with particular interest in the treatment of behavioral aspects of people with dementia.

Herbert Gooden II, an ordained minister and recovery chaplain, has helped thousands of hurting hearts for over 30 years as an instructor, mentor, and spiritual advisor. His work as a clinical neuromuscular therapist has literally touched over 11,000 of God's children from all over the world. He has personally witnessed positive change facilitated through God's word, love, and compassionate touch. He has inspired many with his passion to restore healing to our fellow Christians and the church.

Dr. Bill Hines has a B.A. in Political Science, an M.A. each in Counseling and Religion from Liberty University, and a D.Min. in Biblical Counseling from Trinity Theological Seminary/University of Liverpool. He is the president of Covenant Ministries, a biblical counseling, education and Christian discipleship ministry in Ft. Worth, Texas. Bill is the author of *Leaving Yesterday Behind* and *Curing the Heart: A Model for Biblical Counseling* (with Dr. Howard Eyrich). He co-authored *The Pursuit of Perfection* with Mark Shaw. Bill and his wife Kathy have five children and four grandchildren and make their home in Ft. Worth, Texas.

Mark Robert Hines has a B.A. in Education, University of Texas, and a MABS from Dallas Theological Seminary. An often sought after speaker to youth, he has been a high school guidance counselor at First Baptist Academy in Dallas, Texas for over 30 years. Mark has served as an elder at Country Bible Church in Kaufman, TX for 37 years. He and his wife Karen have two children and one grandchild and make their home in Scurry, Texas.

Alonza D. Jones, Jr. is the president of BMI (Biblical Marriage Institute) which he founded in 2009 with his wife Vanessa. BMI provides prevention-oriented marriage training and education to married couples and students. He holds a B.A. in business administration from Huntingdon College and a M.A. in biblical counseling from Birmingham Theological Seminary. He is an ordained minister, adjunct seminary professor, and has served as an elder and Bible teacher in his home church.

Tim Keeter serves as an elder at Grace Community Church in Huntsville, AL where he also leads the music team. He is an ACBC certified counselor and conference speaker serving the counseling and discipleship ministries of his church. Tim and his wife Carmen have three children.

Dr. Tim Mullet studied biblical counseling at The Master's College and The Southern Baptist Theological Seminary, earning his B.A. and M.Div. respectively. He currently teaches and counsels at Philadelphia Baptist Church.

Dr. Randall J. Price holds a Th.M. from Dallas Theological Seminary in Old Testament and Semitic Languages, and a Ph.D. from the University of Texas at Austin in Middle Eastern Studies with a concentration in Jewish studies and biblical archaeology. Randall is the founder and president of World of the Bible Ministries, Inc. and is Distinguished Research Professor and Executive Director of the Center for Judaic Studies at Liberty University Lynchburg, Virginia. He has served as director of excavations on the Qumran Plateau in Israel since 2002. Among his numerous articles and books are, *Secrets of the Dead Sea Scrolls, Searching for the Original Bible, The Temple in Bible Prophecy, Jerusalem in Prophecy, The Stones Cry Out* and a commentary on Ezekiel and Daniel in the *Popular Bible Prophecy Commentary* (Harvest House). Dr. Price has led over 75 tours of Israel and the Middle East. He and his wife Beverly are parents and grandparents and divide their time between Lynchburg, VA and San Marcos, TX.

Philip Price, BS, R.Ph, is a clinical pharmacist and biblical counselor. He is married with three children and is an elder at CrossLife Church (An Acts 29 Church) in Spartanburg, SC.

Dr. C. Jeffrey Robinson, Sr., holds a Ph.D. from The Southern Baptist Theological Seminary. He is an editor with the Gospel Coalition and serves as adjunct professor of church history for The Southern Baptist Theological Coalition in Louisville, Ky.

Dr. Mark E. Shaw holds a D.Min. in biblical counseling. He is the founder of Truth in Love Ministries and serves as pastor and executive director of Vision of Hope, a ministry of Faith Church Lafayette, Indiana. He is certified with the Association of Certified Biblical Counselors, International Association of Biblical Counselors, and also holds an international Alcohol and Drug Counselor certification. Two of his popular publications are *Addiction Proof Parenting: Biblical Prevention Strategies* and *Strength in Numbers: The Team Approach to Biblical Counseling*, which are now garnering international interest and have been translated into Korean and Romanian, respectively.

Steve Standridge's missionary experience began in Rome, Italy. His higher education was received at Cedarville University and Northwest Baptist Seminary. During seminary he also served as youth pastor in Seattle, WA. From 1986 to 2005 Steve served as director of the the Isola Conference and Discipleship Center in central Italy. Since 2005, Steve, his wife Stephanie, with their children Simeon and Elisa, have been involved in partnering with Italian churches to train the next generation of leaders.

Dr. Deric Thomas, B.A. in Biblical Studies Southeastern Bible College, M.A., M.Div. Southern Baptist Theological Seminary. He is the pastor of Christ Fellowship Church in Gadsden, AL. Having served in several ministries of preaching and teaching the Word of God, he also serves as adjunct faculty for The New Orleans Baptist Seminary Extension Center in Birmingham and Rainsville. Deric and his wife Heather have four children and reside in Gadsden, AL.

Dr. David M. Tyler is the director of Gateway Biblical Counseling and Training Center, dean of the Biblical Counseling Department of Master's International School of Divinity, adjunct instructor at Calvary Bible College and Theological Seminary and president of the American Academy of Biblical Counselors.

Andy Wisner is the church planter and senior pastor of New Life Baptist Church in Harvest, AL, where he ministers with his wife Vicki. He is an ACBC biblical counselor with a love for teaching, and has taught theology and biblical counseling around the globe.

Dr. Jeffrey H. Young, D. Min. B.C., M.A.B.C , Birmingham Theological Seminary. Chaplain, Briarwood Christian School, Birmingham, Alabama.